North Y

Mounta... Bining

Moorland Trails

VERTEBRATE PUBLISHING

Design and production by Vertebrate Publishing, Sheffield
www.v-publishing.co.uk

North York Moors
MountainBiking
Moorland Trails

Written by
Tony Harker

Photography by **John Coefield**

North York Moors
MountainBiking
Moorland Trails

ISBN: 978-1-906148-08-9

Cover photo: **Tony Harker riding Rosedale singletrack.**
All Photography by **John Coefield.**

Design by Nathan Ryder.
www.**v-publishing**.co.uk

All maps reproduced by permission of Ordnance Survey on behalf of The Controller of Her Majesty's Stationery Office.
© Crown Copyright. 100025218

MIX
Paper from responsible sources
FSC® C016973
www.fsc.org

PLEASE GIVE WAY TO HORSES AND PEDESTRIANS.

Download free Sat Nav Point of Interest files from www.**v-outdoor**.co.uk

Contents

Introduction

The north east of England's steel and chemical industrial heritage is well documented and this may be the image that springs to mind if you have never visited the area. However, just a 20 minute drive from the heart of Teesside lies England's largest expanse of heather moorland. This is more than just a wilderness of expansive, outstanding natural beauty. With hundreds of miles of tracks and bridleways the North York Moors is undoubtedly one of England's top locations for XC mountain biking.

Wherever you ride on the moors, you will find panoramic views, endless tracts of rich, purple heather, valley-sides filled with bracken, bilberries and drystone walls bounding the traditional farmlands. The downhills are short in comparison with the neighbouring Dales, but they are numerous and challenging, as are the many singletrack bridleways and miles of moorland tracks. If you like hard ascents, the moors present some of the steepest in the country. If you do visit the moors with your bikes, please consider and respect other users and help to maintain a good relationship between tourists and locals.

Note that the tracks on the moors can change quickly. After a day of pouring rain they can become soft, tiresome and energy-sapping. But many dry out quickly, and what was a tiresome slog after the rain soon becomes a fast, dust-spitting blast. Visitors should also note that, during the summer months, the heather can become very dry and susceptible to fire so do take great care.

There are numerous routes and variations on routes – far too many to include in a single guidebook. The routes in this guide are just a selection of some of the best the moors have to offer. If you need to refuel, there is an abundance of traditional pubs and tearooms around the moors, all of which, in my experience, welcome bikers.

The moors are moody and majestic, and still hold a deep feel of their ancient heritage, which any visitor should sense strengthened as you ride by the visible legacy of the many ancient standing stones, monuments and burial mounds. Come and enjoy mountain biking on the North York Moors. I guarantee you will want to come back for more!

Tony Harker
www.muddybums.org.uk

Acknowledgements

Acknowledgements from the Author...

I would like to thank Sam McIntyre, Steve Tilly and Rob Linklater for their help, encouragement and company while compiling this guide. There were no complaints regardless of the weather conditions, the worst being a 25mph blizzard on Rudland Rigg! A huge thanks also to my wife Kay for never complaining about my absence or the endless washing of muddy kit.

...and from VP

Thanks to Tim and Kim Russon, Jon Barton and Tom Fenton for helping out with photos and route testing, and to Tony for producing such a great selection of rides. Thanks also to Ian at Stif for loaning us the incredible Ibis Mojo! (It's an amazing trail bike – you really should demo/buy one...!) Thanks to John Coefield for editing, photography and proofreading.

How to Use This Book

Riding in the North York Moors

The North York Moors aren't the biggest hills in the UK but that doesn't mean they aren't packed with quality mountain biking – climbs and descents. It's got to be one of the most beautiful areas in the UK and the riding is lush too; fine moorland single-track, fast forest doubletrack, steep and rocky descents and lung-busting climbs.

Bear in mind this is moorland and it's quite easy to find yourself some distance from car, café and help. One area of the high moorland plateau can be indistinguishable from another when the fog and bad weather roll in, so don't rely on this guidebook alone, especially in adverse weather conditions. Take a map and compass and know how to use them. Other than that, just enjoy some of the best riding in the UK!

The routes

This guide contains 20 of the best circular rides in the North York Moors plus a one-way jaunt thrown in for good measure. The aim is to showcase what the area has to offer – it's not just Dalby in North Yorkshire you know! Some of the rides are just as good in reverse and many get better on the second and third ride as you learn the best bits.

Classics are fairly short (but not necessarily easy). **Epics** are a little longer and require that bit more effort. **Enduros** step things up again and **Killers** are pretty self-explanatory.

Grades

Routes, climbs and descents are graded blue, red and black, in a similar system to that used at several of the trail centres around the UK.

▲ = Easy   ▲ = Moderate   ▲ = Hard

The grades are based on average conditions – good weather and not too wet and muddy. In a drought the routes will feel easier, in the depths of winter, harder. Grades consider technicality, length, climbs, navigation, and remoteness – so one 'black' route might be a short all-out technical test while another could be a big endurance challenge with tricky navigation. As ever, these grades are subjective. How you find a particular route, downhill or climb will be dictated by your own levels of fitness and skill.

Directions & Accuracy

While every effort has been made to ensure accuracy within the directions in this guide, things change and we are unable to guarantee that every detail will be correct. Please treat stated distances as guidelines. **Please exercise caution if a direction appears at odds with the route on the ground. A comparison between direction and map should see you on the right track.**

Rights of Way

Countryside access in the UK hasn't been particularly kind to cyclists, although things are improving. We have 'right of way' on bridleways (blue arrows on signs) and byways (red arrows). However, having 'right of way' doesn't actually mean having the right of way, just that we're allowed to ride there – so give way to walkers and horse riders. We're also allowed to ride on green lanes and some unclassified roads, although the only way to determine which are legal and which aren't is to check with the local countryside authority. Obviously, cycle routes are also in.

The very understanding Forestry Commission generally allows cyclists to use its land (again, you'll need to check with them first to be sure). You must, however, obey all signs, especially those warning of forestry operations – a fully loaded logging truck will do more than scuff your frame...

Everything else is out of bounds (unless, of course, the landowner says otherwise). Riding illegally can upset walkers, (who have every right to enjoy their day); is, in many cases, technically classed as trespass (meaning you could be prosecuted for any damage caused). **Please don't do it.**

Not all tracks are signed, so it's not always obvious whether that great-looking trail you want to follow is an illegal footpath or a legal bridleway. That's why it's a good idea to carry a map with you on every ride.

The Bike

Any half-decent mountain bike will be fine (try and avoid a '£99 special'). A full suspension bike will add comfort and control. A lightweight race number will make hills easier and something with a bit of travel will help on technical descents. We'd pick a compromise somewhere between the three, depending on your personal preferences.

Check everything's working – you won't be going uphill fast if your gears seize but equally you'll be a little quicker than planned if your brakes fail coming down. Pump the tyres up, check nothing's about to wear through and make sure that everything that should be tight is tight.

Essential Kit

Helmet
"The best helmet is the one that you're wearing". Make sure it fits, you're wearing it correctly and that it won't move in a crash.

Clothing
You need to get your clothing right if you want to stay comfortable on a bike, especially in bad weather. The easiest way to do this is to follow a layering system. Begin with clothing made from 'technical' synthetic or wool fabrics that will wick the sweat away from your body and then dry quickly, keeping you dry and warm. Stay away from cotton – it absorbs moisture and holds onto it. If it's chilly, an insulating layer will keep you warm, and a wind/waterproof layer on the outside protects from the elements. Layers can then be removed or added to suit the conditions. Padded shorts are more comfortable, but the

UK's No1 Performance Mountain Bike Store
77 OTLEY ROAD • HEADINGLEY • LEEDS • LS6 3PS • 0113 225 1111 • WWW.STIF.CO.UK

  ibis **Orange**

amount of lycra on display is down to you. Baggy shorts, full length tights and trousers are all available to match the conditions. Set off a little on the cold side – you'll soon warm up. Don't leave the warm clothes behind though, as the weather can turn quickly.

Gloves
Gloves ward off blisters and numb hands and help keep your fingers warm. They also provide a surprising amount of protection when you come off.

Footwear
Flat pedals/clips-ins – it's your call. Make sure you can walk in the shoes and that they have sufficient tread for you to do so. Consider overshoes if it's chilly.

Other essentials
As mentioned, take any necessary spares, tools, tube and pump, spare clothes, first aid kit, food and water. Stop short of the kitchen sink, as you'll still want to be able to actually ride your bike.

You'll need something to carry this lot in. We'd suggest a hydration pack, as they allow you to drink on the move and keep excess weight off the bike.

Night Riding

Night riding is ace! It's possible to enjoy an after-work ride in the depths of winter in your favourite off-road playground. But it's a completely different ball game and (hardly surprisingly) there are a few risks to be aware of.

Lights and batteries
Invest carefully in a lighting system. Consider battery life, weight, number/type of bulbs and power. Fully charge your battery before a ride (sounds like common sense, until you forget). Carry a secondary light source (such as a head torch) for emergencies (it's surprising what you can ride with a commuter light if you have to, although it isn't much fun). Pack a rear light for road sections and keep it clean.

Route planning and safety

Choose your ride on the basis of battery life. Time it yourself, don't necessarily rely on the manufacturer's information. Allow extra time – you'll be slower in the dark. Stay on ground that you are familiar with at first (night-time navigation in unfamiliar territory demands military expertise) and not too far from home. Ride with a friend. Watch out for the werewolves. Tell someone you're out. **Ride within your limits – trees loom up very quickly in the dark!**

General Safety

The ability to read a map, navigate in poor visibility and to understand weather warnings is essential. Don't head out in bad weather, unless you're confident and capable of doing so.

Some of the routes described point you at tough climbs and steep descents that can potentially be very dangerous. Too much exuberance on a steep descent in the middle of nowhere and you could be in more than a spot of bother, especially if you're alone. Consider your limitations and relative fragility.

Be self-sufficient. Carry food and water, spares, a tube and a pump. Consider a first-aid kit. Even if it's warm, the weather could turn, so take a wind/waterproof. Think about what could happen on an enforced stop. Pack lights if you could finish in the dark.

If you're riding solo, think about the seriousness of an accident – you might be without help for a very long time. Tell someone where you're going, when you'll be back and tell them once you are back. Take a mobile phone if you have one, but don't expect a signal. And **don't** call out the ambulance because you've grazed your knee.

Riding in a group is safer (ambitious overtaking manoeuvres excepted) and often more fun, but don't leave slower riders too far behind and give them a minute for a breather when they've caught up. Allow extra time for a group ride, as you'll inevitably stop and chat. You might need an extra top if you're standing around for a while. Ride within your ability, make sure you can slow down fast and give way to other users. Bells might be annoying, but they work. If you can't bring yourself to bolt one on, a polite 'excuse me' should be fine. **On hot, sunny days, slap on some Factor 30+ and ALWAYS WEAR YOUR HELMET!**

In the Event of an Accident

In the event of an accident requiring immediate assistance: Dial 999 and ask for POLICE or AMBULANCE. If you can supply the services with a grid reference of exactly where you are it should help to speed up their response time.

Rules of the (Off) Road

1. Always ride on legal trails.
2. Ride considerately – give way to horses and pedestrians.
3. Don't spook animals.
4. Ride in control – you don't know who's around the next corner.
5. Leave gates as you find them – if you're unsure, shut them.
6. Keep the noise down and don't swear loudly when you fall off in front of walkers.
7. Leave no trace – take home everything you took out.
8. Keep water sources clean – don't take toilet stops near streams.
9. Enjoy the countryside and respect its life and work.

Planning Your Ride

1. Consider the ability/experience of each rider in your group. Check the weather forecast. How much time do you have available? Now choose your route.
2. Study the route description before setting off, and cross-reference it with the relevant map.
3. Bear in mind everything we've suggested about safety, clothing, spares and food and drink.
4. Get out there and get dirty.

Maps & Symbols

This is the first Vertebrate guidebook to use Ordnance Survey maps. They are the most commonly used, easy to read and many people are happy using them. If you're not familiar with OS maps and are unsure of what the symbols mean, you can download a free map legend from www.v-outdoor.co.uk

Here's a guide to the symbols and abbreviations we use on the maps and in our directions:

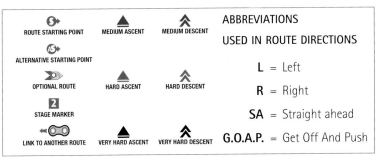

			ABBREVIATIONS
ROUTE STARTING POINT	MEDIUM ASCENT	MEDIUM DESCENT	USED IN ROUTE DIRECTIONS
ALTERNATIVE STARTING POINT			
OPTIONAL ROUTE	HARD ASCENT	HARD DESCENT	**L** = Left
STAGE MARKER			**R** = Right
			SA = Straight ahead
LINK TO ANOTHER ROUTE	VERY HARD ASCENT	VERY HARD DESCENT	**G.O.A.P.** = Get Off And Push

The Ordnance Survey maps in this book should serve you well for this selection of rides, but if you are not familiar with the area, or if conditions are poor and you need a back-up, you can't beat carrying the real thing. The following OS maps cover the North York Moors National Park:

Ordnance Survey Landranger Maps
93 – Middlesbrough
94 – Whitby & Esk Dale
99 – Northallerton & Ripon
100 – Malton & Pickering
101 – Scarborough

Ordnance Survey Explorer Maps
OL26 – North York Moors Western Area
OL27 – North York Moors Eastern Area
299 – Ripon & Boroughbridge

To help you find the start of each route, you can download free Sat Nav Point of Interest files from www.v-outdoor.co.uk

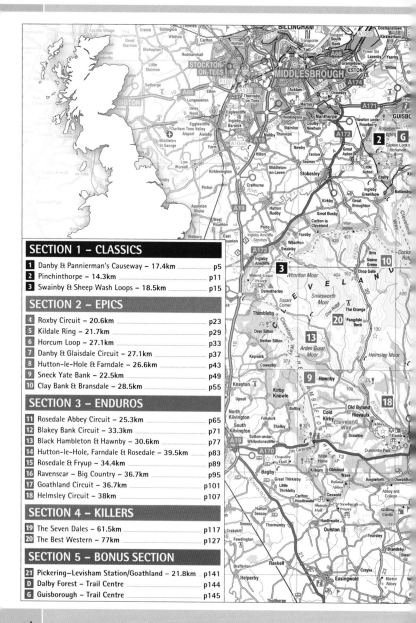

North York Moors
MountainBiking
Area Map & Route Finder

SECTION 1

Classics

A quick blast after work, a night loop you can finish before your lights die, or a ride to squeeze in when time is short. That's a classic. They're not long, but that doesn't mean they're easy... Good, solid rides that all riders should enjoy.

Classics
sponsored by

www.muddybums.org.uk

01 Danby & Pannierman's Causeway

17.4km

Introduction

The moors are home to many ancient paths or causeways, sometimes known as 'trods'. The Pannierman's Causeway is one of these and although there is only about 200 yards of the ancient pathway exposed, it offers riders an unusual section of singletrack. Thought to have been laid by monks in the 12th Century, this causeway is one of many on the moors used by monks and their pack-horses in their travels from settlement to settlement to trade.

The Ride

Predominantly off-road, this route offers a variety of track riding, most of which is easy to follow, making it easy to enjoy the views across to Fryup and Danby Dale from the bridleway above Castleton Pits. Our route begins by following the Esk Valley towards Commondale. We bypass Commondale by the bridleway that cuts up to the road, but we could continue into Commondale for refreshments at the Cleveland Inn or the Old Post Office Tea Room. From the road, the route turns east and onto the sandy track towards Gerrick Moor, where a little more road brings us to the Pannierman's Causeway. The best bit of the route, it is an stretch of ancient, paved singletrack with views straight ahead towards Danby Rigg. A fine bridleway leads us around the edge of Castleton Pits. A rough doubletrack downhill leads to a quick blast back to the car park on the road.

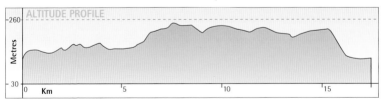

ALTITUDE PROFILE

Metres

260

30

0   Km   5   10   15

DANBY & PANNIERMAN'S CAUSEWAY   **GRADE:** ▲

TOTAL DISTANCE: 17.4KM » **TOTAL ASCENT:** 344M » **START REFERENCE:** NZ 717084 » **SATNAV:** YO21 2NB
START/FINISH: DANBY LODGE CAR PARK » **PARKING:** DANBY LODGE CAR PARK (PAY AND DISPLAY)
CAFÉ: THE MOORS TEAROOM, DANBY LODGE TEL: 01287 660362; STONEHOUSE BAKERY, DANBY TEL: 01287 660006
PUBLIC HOUSE: DUKE OF WELLINGTON, DANBY TEL: 01287 660351; THE CLEVELAND INN, COMMONDALE TEL: 01287 660214

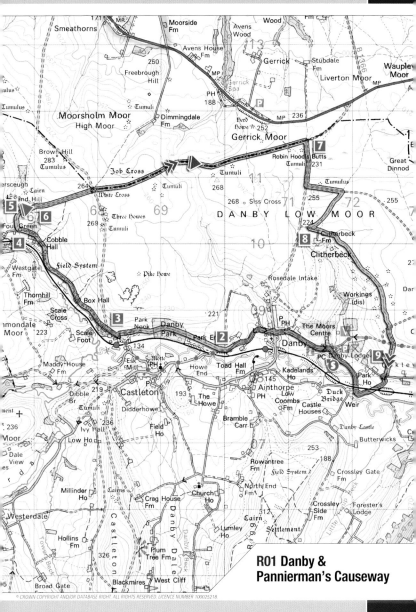

**R01 Danby &
Pannierman's Causeway**

Directions – Danby &
Pannierman's Causeway

➏ Turn **R** out of the car park and follow the road into Danby village. At the crossroads go **SA** onto the road to Castleton and follow this for 700m. After the road bends right before heading downhill to the left turn **R** uphill onto a driveway. Turn immediately **L** off the driveway onto doubletrack bridleway with a wall on the right.

2 Follow this bridleway east to Danby Park woods ignoring two forks to the right. Pass through the gate into the woods, onto a muddy track for 550m and through another gate out of the woods. Follow this track with a fence and then a wall on the left and go **SA** through two more gates, over a cattle grid and to the Castleton road. Take care here and be sure to be ready to stop. You cannot check for traffic until you are right up to the road.

3 Turn **R** uphill for a short lung burst and then at the first bend turn **L** onto a bridleway with a wall on left. Follow this fast, hard track past Box Hall as far as a second set of buildings and bear **R** at the fork up another short climb to the woods. Go through the woods and continue for 160m where the walls open out.

4 Turn **R** uphill to a gate with a *Bridleway* sign. (Opposite gate on left with *Footpath* sign and before the gate at the next wall). Pass through the gate onto a wide grassy track keeping the wall to the left. The track becomes a more defined singletrack. After 180m cross a ditch and the track starts to bear more to the right and steeply uphill to a single gate in the wall on the horizon. (Top right corner with wire fence).

5 Pass through the gate and turn **R** onto singletrack with a little pavement. After 50m the track bears left away from the wall onto a wide doubletrack. There is a boulder here on each side of the track. (**SA** would lead you into a bog!) Follow to the road.

6 Turn **R** onto the road and continue to the T-junction. Continue **SA** onto another bridleway that begins with broken tarmac changing to sandstone further on. As you climb over the first brow the view to the NE opens up over towards Boulby potash mines and the North Sea. Continue on this track past Siss Cross Hill to the Danby road.

7 Turn **R** at the road and then after 650m at brow of hill turn **L** onto narrow tarmac lane. Follow this lane for 600m into the 'saddle'. A *Bridleway* sign on the left marks the point where the bridleway crosses the road. Turn **R** onto the Pannierman's

Causeway singletrack in a shallow gully and follow this track as it bears first SW and then S towards Clitherbeck Farm. This track soon becomes pavement and leads onto the bridleway near the farm. Watch out for the ditches at the end of the pavement and just before the farm.

8 Turn **L** onto the bridleway and continue **SA** ignoring the right turn to the farm. At the bottom where the track bears right (footpath) leave the track and go **SA** picking up a singletrack to the right of a shallow gully. Stay on this track to rejoin the main track after 170m. Turn **L** and follow to road. At the road go **SA** to T-junction.

9 Go **SA** through the gate opposite and down a wide rough, doubletrack, walled on both sides. Turn **R** at the bottom onto a narrow lane and follow this under the railway to another junction. Turn **R** and follow the road back to the car park.

Introduction

A mix of forest trails and typical moors tracks, this is an ideal route if you don't have much time, or for after a shift at work. The section down to Roseberry Common is technical, and is something of a white knuckle ride if you're not a downhill-lemming.

The Ride

A nice easy start heads through the woods and over open fields to Hutton Village. The uphill starts with a heart-pumping climb into the forest, with another burst to bring you out under Highcliffe Nab and a great view over the Eston Hills. An easier climb takes you up to the moor and a rough but fast descent into Sleddale. Another short, sharp lung-buster brings you out over the Lonsdale Plantations. Recent felling has opened up fantastic views over the Cleveland Hills. More moorland riding follows before diving back into the forest for short but sweet pine-lined singletrack. A steep, rocky drop leads to Roseberry Common and then a swoop over the Common back into the woods. Finish with a short 'black' section weaving in the trees and a fast finish on forest track.

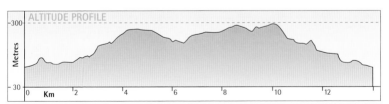

PINCHINTHORPE **GRADE:** ▲»▲

TOTAL DISTANCE: 14.3KM » **TOTAL ASCENT:** 384M » **START GRID REFERENCE:** NZ 584152 » **SATNAV:** TS14 8HD
START/FINISH: PINCHINTHORPE VISITOR CENTRE, GUISBOROUGH » **PARKING:** PINCHINTHORPE VISITOR CENTRE CAR PARK
CAFÉ: PLENTY IN GUISBOROUGH » **PUBLIC HOUSE:** PLENTY IN GUISBOROUGH

Directions – Pinchinthorpe

➊ Leave the car park at a single gate near visitor centre and turn **L**. Follow this track to a right turn 50m after two ponds on the left. After 20m turn **L** at T-junction on forest road. Follow this for a further 250m down the hill to another junction. Turn **L** onto a rough farm road across the fields. This will take you to the Hutton Village road.

2 Turn **R** at the road and follow through the village. **SA** at the gate on the forest edge, and up the hill. At the top of the hill turn **L** onto a wide forest road. Continue past a cleared area and then keep **SA** at the fork where a track goes right, signposted *Highcliffe Farm*. At the top of a sharp climb the view to the north opens up. Continue as far as a metal gate under Highcliffe Nab.

3 Just before the gate take track to the **R** marked with a *Bridleway* sign. Continue for 60m to two gates. Take the single gate **SA** onto a grassy track with fence on the right and gorse on the left. **SA** at the next two gates, and then 100m to the moor gate in the wall.

4 Go **SA** at gate onto doubletrack. After 50m turn right at track. After another 50m take **R** fork staying on main track. Keep on this track down into Sleddale to the farm lane at the bottom. Turn **R** onto the lane and follow this over the stream on a sharp bend and up a steep climb to Percy Cross Rigg. Turn **R** and ride for 850m to a gate.

5 At the gate ignore track to left and go **SA** up a sandstone track marked with a *Bridleway* post. Pass a shelter at the top and continue down to forest edge through two gates.

6 Take the gravelled bridleway left, along forest edge **or** take singletrack into the trees, marked with a black arrow on a post - 300m of pine covered track winding through the trees; after 250m turn **L** at signpost and join the main track at the fence. Turn **R** and follow it for 300m just past a right bend to a *Bridleway* signpost. and gate on left.

7 Stay on this track over the moor and onto a gate at the corner of a wall. Go through the gate and follow the bridleway that becomes paved downhill. This is technical, where paved, with regular water gullies. Continue along the wall down a steeper, paved section to a gate in the wall on the left.

8 Turn **R** at the gate onto a wide bridleway. Stay on this bridleway through two more gates to the forest corner. After the wall corner turn **L** after about 20m at a wooden post with a black arrow. (About 300m after the last gate). This is winding singletrack but eroded in places. At the bottom, turn **L** on the forest track.

9 Follow this track for 1.2km to a gate and back onto the track you started on. Stay with the main track past a house on the left and take the next right then left onto the walkway track back to the visitor centre.

R02 Pinchinthorpe

03 Swainby & Sheep Wash Loops

18.5km (Bottom loop, 10.5km top loop, 7.5km)

Introduction

This versatile route can be ridden as one larger figure-of-eight, or as two shorter loops. You could start in Swainby and ride the whole figure-of-eight, or just the 'bottom' loop, or start at the 'Sheep Wash' near Cod Beck Reservoir and again ride the whole route or just the 'top' loop. The directions are written with the Swainby start. Note that you won't find anything on the map named the Sheep Wash – it's the name given to a well-known local beauty spot near Cod Beck Reservoir. It's lovely too: the scenery is magnificent and the riding easy.

The Ride

We leave Swainby village heading south on the Osmotherley road to the Scarth Nick Gap leading on to the beauty spot known locally as the Sheep Wash, close to Cod Beck Reservoir. From here, we take the track over the ford and onto the Roman road, bearing right into the forest and dropping down to the reservoir, following the track to the Osmotherley Road. At the top of the village, we start a long, gentle uphill, distinguished by a 180° panorama of the heather clad hills to take your mind off the climb. From the top, we follow a wide, firm paved track back down to Scarth Nick – fast but not steep, and there are plenty of rocky drainage channels to hone your jump skills. We enter Scarth Nick Woods for a steep descent on a wide stepped drop and follow the swooping bridleway through the woods to the ford over Scugdale Beck. Singletrack riding leads us around the woods below Live Moor and onto the lane through Faceby. The last leg takes us from Faceby around the north side of Whorl Hill over meadows and crop fields leading back to Swainby.

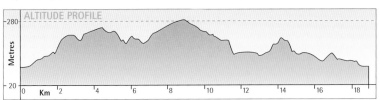

ALTITUDE PROFILE

SWAINBY & SHEEP WASH LOOPS   **GRADE:** ▲

TOTAL DISTANCE: 18.5KM (10.5KM/7.5KM) » **TOTAL ASCENT:** 503M (290M/190M) » **START GRID REFERENCE:** NZ 477020 **SATNAV:** DL6 3ED » **START/FINISH:** SWAINBY VILLAGE OR SHEEP WASH » **PARKING:** ROADSIDE IN SWAINBY, OR COD BECK RESERVOIR » **CAFÉ:** COFFEE POT, OSMOTHERLEY TEL: 01609 883 536 » **PUBLIC HOUSE:** THE MINERS ARMS TEL: 01642 700 457, THE BLACKSMITHS ARMS TEL: 01642 700 303, THE BLACK HORSE TEL: 01642 700 436 (ALL SWAINBY)

Directions – Swainby & Sheep Wash Loops

↪ Head south (west side of stream) out of Swainby on the Osmotherley road onto a short but steep climb to the cattle grid at the Scarth Nick gap.

2 Continue for a further 900m to the bend at the Sheep Wash. Turn **L** off the road and cross the ford onto a wide, steep but short climb, for most will be a **G.O.A.P.** (**G**et **O**ff **A**nd **P**ush). Continue 1km and turn **R** at the *Route 65* sign onto a firm forest track. At the bottom of the hill turn **L**, and then **R** after another 100m and follow through to the reservoir dam.

3 At the far side of dam follow the track around a left bend to a gate leading to the road. Keep **SA** towards Osmotherley. After 1km turn **R** onto a narrow lane. Follow this for 1.7km to a sharp left bend. Go **SA** through gate onto double farm track and then **SA** at single gate onto paved bridleway track. Follow the bridleway downhill, keeping right at junction with footpath and *Bridleway* sign near the bottom.

4 Turn **L** onto the road back to the cattle grid at Scarth Nick. Just past the cattle grid turn **R** though a single gate into the woods. Follow singletrack, which shortly joins a forest track, and keep left at junction after 600m. Keep to track down stepped drop.

5 To continue turn **L** and follow bridleway, sharp **R** before gate.

> **OR** *Alternatively, to finish early turn **L**, through gate and **SA** to Swainby.

6 Back on the main route, stay with this rolling track for 1.1km, keeping **SA** to gate. After gate turn **L** around tree and down though the field to the gate at the bottom.

7 **SA** at gate over ford and turn **L** onto lane. Follow the lane to the Scugdale road and cross straight over to gate signposted *Cleveland Way & Carlton Bank*. Follow firm singletrack along edge of woods, **SA** at gate. After another 250m turn **L** through single gate into field onto rough singletrack. (Often difficult to ride due to horse traffic.)

8 Keep to the track parallel with fence to right. Rejoin the forest at single gate in corner of field. Keep left shortly after gate onto a nice bit of singletrack running down to another gate. **SA** at gate crossing the field at angle to the gate at the far side.

9 Turn **L** onto lane and follow through Faceby. 50m after road junction and Sutton Arms turn **L** onto lane (opposite red iron gate). Keep **SA** at gate passing the chicken huts and follow to farm. Turn **R** and then **L** around the bungalow. Follow the track keeping straight ahead at all gates. Turn **R** onto the lane to return to Swainby.

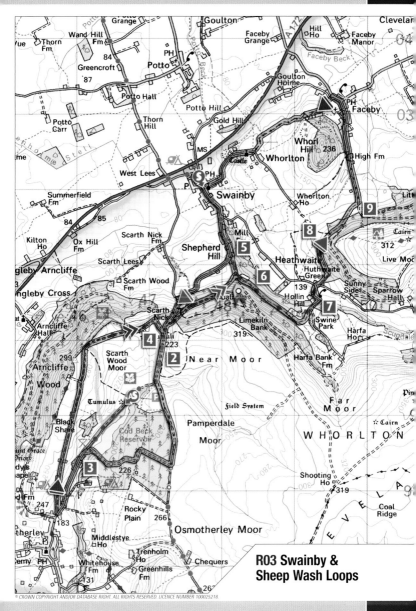

R03 Swainby & Sheep Wash Loops

SECTION 2

Epics

Getting longer, Epics require that bit more time and effort. The difficulty varies but all feature a mix of fast, technical and tough riding that covers some interesting ground and is not to be underestimated. Allow a few hours and enjoy some of the best riding the moors have to offer.

Epics

sponsored by **bike**magic.com

04 Roxby Circuit

Introduction

This ride takes us a little off the beaten track over Roxby Moor. The riding is fairly easy but we must be careful with the navigation and attention to route detail. After the first and only real climb, up Lealholm Bank, we are rewarded with stunning views up the valley and a cracking mile of fast singletrack back over Roxby Moor. The stepping stone crossing over the Esk should only be attempted when water levels are low!

The Ride

Turn off the A171 onto the lane to Tranmire Farm. Easy riding and careful navigation take us over the ford at Haredale Beck and Green Houses. The riding becomes more pastoral with some road work. There are some great views into the Esk Valley before we drop to the River Esk and a stepping stones crossing. The ford here can be too wide and fast to cross by bike! Some demanding short climbs and soft riding bring us to the farm lane and easy riding alongside the Esk, coming out into Lealholm village. We climb Lealholm Bank to Lealholm Side and then onto the Lealholm Moor track towards Danby Beacon. Turn north onto some wonderful singletrack that crosses Roxby Moor before picking up the Tranmire lane again back to the reservoir.

ROXBY CIRCUIT GRADE: ▲

TOTAL DISTANCE: 20.6KM » **TOTAL ASCENT:** 403M » **START GRID REFERENCE:** NZ 755128
SATNAV: TS13 4TP (CLOSEST) » **START/FINISH:** SCALING DAM » **PARKING:** SCALING DAM CAR PARK
CAFÉ: SHEPHERDS HALL, LEALHOLM TEL: 01947 897361 » **PUBLIC HOUSE:** THE BOARD INN, LEALHOLM TEL: 01947 897279

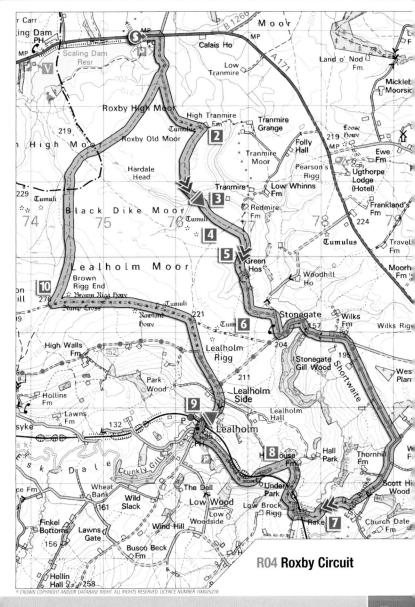

Directions – Roxby Circuit

➤ Turn **R** out of car park onto the A171 for only 200m and then turn **R** into lane to Tranmire. Stay on this lane for 2.5km to High Tranmire Farm.

2 Just 10m before the farm gate turn **R** onto wide track bridleway, becoming rutted, running parallel with wall to left. Ignore track to right and keep **SA** until the track makes a sharp left turn to a new fence. Follow the cleared track down the right hand side of the fence until a kink in the fence and a gate. Go through the gate onto wide track, becoming gravelled, dropping steeply through a gate and over ford.

3 Climb steeply to a point at the top of the climb where the track turns sharp right, turning grassy. Leave the track and go over to the wall in front. Turn **R** at the wall and follow a narrow sheep track for almost 200m to the wall corner. (This is the bridleway. If you stay on the main track you will go off course).

4 At the wall corner look SE over the moor and pick out the top of two gate posts. This is the direction you need to head. You should be able to pick your way along another narrow sheep track for 200m over the moor to the gate. If visibility is poor, you may need to take a bearing.

5 Go **SA** at gate with fence on right changing to wall. Go though the right-hand gate in the corner of field onto a grassy track between two walls (*Bridleway* sign on gate). After 100m take the right hand gate of two and follow a grassy track with wall on right. Follow the track down the hill, keeping **left** at forks and turn **L** onto farm road around the front of the farm. Turn **R** onto lane.

6 Follow the lane bending left up the hill. Turn **R** at junction and after 300m turn **L** at a T-junction. Drop down the hill swing right over the stream and climb up to the next turning with a blue *Route 52* sign. Turn **R** and follow for 1.5km, turning **R** at the next junction. Pass the first bridleway on the right to farm and take the next **R** down a narrow lane keeping left of farmhouse. Track turns soft for the rest of the descent to the River Esk.

7 Cross the river via the stepping stones or the ford if safe to do so. Follow the track bending right past Rake Farm and then **R** onto lane. Take this lane down a short steep muddy drop to the ford (there is a footbridge to left if you need it). Keep left after the ford along a very soft and rutted track. This track turns right up a rough road over the railway and then up to Hill House Farm.

8   Pass the farm along the lane for 200m. Turn **L** onto bridleway head SW over the brow of the hill. **SA** at gate down very muddy track next to fence, swing right and then left under railway bridge. Pass through the farmyard and turn **R** onto bridleway. Firm riding for 1km to Lealholm.

9   Turn **R** at road and climb the hill to Lealholm Side to the junction signposted *Oakley Heights*. Turn **L** here for 600m to bend. Leave the road and go **SA** onto dirt track. Turn left after 400m and follow this wide stony track for 2km to a point where a bridleway crosses the track. Turn **R** onto doubletrack taking the right-hand of two tracks.

10   Follow this track, which becomes singletrack in parts, for almost 2km to a flat wide grassy area. Keep slightly right onto sandstone track. Ignore track to right and follow through to the lane. Turn **L** and then **L** again on A171 and **L** into car park.

Introduction

This is a short route, mostly off road once the climb past Park Nab has been achieved. The peaceful remoteness at the head of Baysdale and the packhorse bridge over Hograh Beck are most enjoyable, while the singletracks over Hograh Moor and Kildale Moor will test your technical skills. Finally the old mine chimney in Leven Dale provides a little historical interest.

The Ride

We climb past Park Nab on a long pull up the lane to Battersby Moor and ride over Ingleby Moor, before dropping into the head of Baysdale, a wonderful spot for a few quiet moments. A sharp climb out of Baysdale brings us to some easy track riding in preparation for a wickedly fast descent to the packhorse bridge over Hograh Beck. Starting off rocky, a single-track crosses Hograh Moor and is followed by a steep descent to Hob Hole. Follow the stony bridleway into Baysdale, watching the valley open up as we make our way along the rough track. A short climb and more singletrack over Kildale Moor follow, before a short energy-sapping ride down the field leading to the old chimney in Leven Dale. A last spurt of energy is required to get up to Warren Farm before the final road descent back to Kildale.

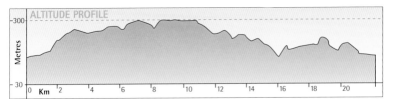

KILDALE RING	GRADE: ▲

TOTAL DISTANCE: 21.7KM » **TOTAL ASCENT:** 576M » **START GRID REFERENCE:** NZ 604095 » **SATNAV:** YO21 2RH
START/FINISH: STATION CAR PARK, KILDALE » **PARKING:** STATION CAR PARK, KILDALE » **CAFÉ:** GLEBE COTTAGE TEAROOM, KILDALE TEL: 01642 724470 » **PUBLIC HOUSE:** THE CLEVELAND INN, COMMONDALE TEL: 01287 660214; SEVERAL IN GREAT AYTON

Directions – Kildale Ring

➊ Turn **L** out of car park and ride up the lane past Glebe Farm to the T-junction in the village. Turn **R** and then, after 800m, **L** into a narrow lane.

2 Follow this lane for 3km passing Park Nab to the left, all the way to the sharp left bend to Baysdale Abbey. Leave the road at this point and go **SA** on a firm track through a metal gate, followed by a wooden gate after 50m.

3 Stay **SA** after the gate for another 800m and look out for a small cairn on the right where a track goes off to the left. Turn **L** on this track across moor and just after 2km and a short drop turn **R** at junction. Follow this over a small rock bridge to the valley head and a bridge over a stream.

4 Climb the track from the stream, steep at first but levelling quite soon. **SA** over the moor. About 1.4km after the stream, the track bends to right and drops a little to another track. Turn **L** and follow the track over a slight rise and then begin to descend for almost 1km. Look out for a turning off to the right. Slow down and turn **R**. Stay with this track all the way to the packhorse bridge at Great Hograh Beck.

 CAUTION! Just above the bridge the track drops steeply. This is only rideable by the highly skilled. To **avoid** this difficult section, turn **L** above the drop and then **R** to make your way down the side of the drop to the packhorse bridge.

5 Cross the bridge, heading east onto singletrack, which is rocky in parts, but clears up further on. There are two dips to beck crossings and a final blast over the moor to the John Breckon Road. Turn **L** at the road and then **L** again at the next junction. Drop steeply to the ford at Hob Hole. Keep **SA** from the ford up a steep climb to the bridleway opposite the road end to Castleton.

6 Turn **L** at the bridleway. After almost 2km, turn **R** at barn onto singletrack and a short steep climb. 300m after climb, go **SA** at gate and down to single gate.

7 **SA** at gate across a soft field and **SA** at next gate turning **L** past the chimney. **SA** at another gate. Climb farm track up steep bank past Warren Farm and through a gate to lane. Turn **L** for a steep drop and **L** again back to Kildale. Turn **R** in Kildale back to the station car park.

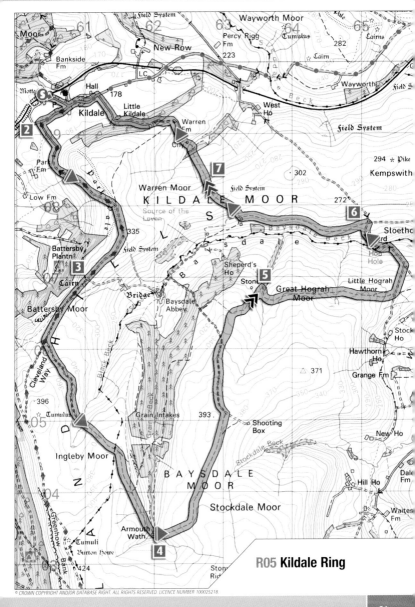

R05 Kildale Ring

Introduction

This is a fairly easy ride with an 8km blast down through Langdale Forest. The ride along the edge of Saltergate Bank has terrific views and there is some nice singletrack to test a beginner's skills.

The Ride

We leave the north end of the car park onto a wide bridleway, before skirting the edge of the woods to the escarpment. We are rewarded with great views all the way along the edge, to the nice little downhill

into Malo Cross. A mix of singletrack leads north to the edge of RAF Fylingdales, where you are guided (!) past by orange markers, before turning onto hard doubletrack along the edge of Langdale Forest. Dive into the forest and join the long, dirt-spitting 8km descent on wide forest road towards Langdale End. Shortly after leaving the forest, we head for Bickley Gate Bank, before ducking back into the forest for more bridleway riding to the fabulous viewpoint at the forest edge. A steady downhill on moorland track brings us to a stiff climb up Newgate Brow. Finally we take the Old Wife's Way back to the car park where we started.

HORCUM LOOP   **GRADE:** ▲

TOTAL DISTANCE: 27.1KM » **TOTAL ASCENT:** 530M » **START GRID REFERENCE:** SE 852938
SATNAV: SALTERGATE/SALTERSGATE **START/FINISH:** HOLE OF HORCUM » **PARKING:** HOLE OF HORCUM CAR PARK (FREE)
CAFÉ: PLENTY IN PICKERING » **PUBLIC HOUSE:** THE MOORCOCK INN, LANGDALE END TEL: 01723 882268; PLENTY IN PICKERING

Directions — Horcum Loop

➊ Go to north end of car park and turn **R** onto a wide bridleway signposted *Cross Cliff 4m*. After 200m, just before a double gate, turn **L** through gate onto singletrack along edge of woods.

➋ After 200m turn **R** through single gate and follow doubletrack along the escarpment. **SA** at gate after 400m and then after another 400m turn **L** onto grassy singletrack angling down Saltergate Bank.

➌ At bottom of hill, turn **L** through gate signposted to *Lilla Cross*. Keep the trees on your right and go **SA** at next gate, following singletrack towards RAF Fylingdales. **SA** at track onto more singletrack marked with orange topped posts. After 700m track bends to right through single gate onto concrete road.

➍ Turn **R** on road and follow down bank over stream and **SA** at gate. Stay on wide stone track keeping trees to right for 2km to fork. Turn **R** into forest. Stay on this forest road for 8km to tarmac lane ignoring all turns offs.

➎ Follow road for 1.5km to junction and turn **R** past monastery signs. Keep **L** after 2.4km and pass toll onto forest drive up Bickley Gate Bank. After 800m from bank top turn **R** onto forest track. After 1km, at fork, bear **R** on bridleway towards viewpoint.

➏ At multiple junction keep **SA** downhill. Beware double gate, turn next **L** onto bridleway, through double gate, pass farm and follow track over the moor for 1.5km. Go **SA** at gate, track swings left, then right with hedge on right. At field corner, turn **L** down to farm at Newgate Foot.

➐ Go through farmyard onto concrete road uphill. Follow wide track for 1.3km back to car park.

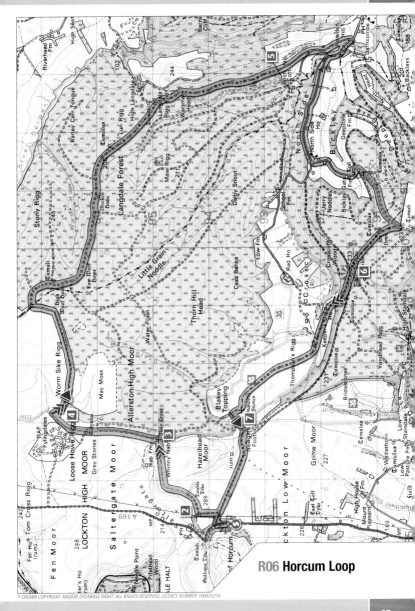

R06 Horcum Loop

07 Danby & Glaisdale Circuit

27.1km

Introduction

This route epitomises all the North York Moors have to offer: there are fast gravel tracks, technical climbs and descents, leg-burning road climbs and brake-burning descents; there's a ford to cool you down and long hills to heat you up, with a high viewpoint at the end to survey the whole route!

The Ride

We follow the road through Danby and Ainthorpe climbing up to Ainthorpe Rigg, and take the singletrack bridleway over the Rigg. Eroded ruts make this a difficult and technical ride to the far edge, but two rock steps at the top and a sweeping singletrack drop into the Little Fryup Valley make it all worthwhile. A long road climb leads to the bridleway around the head of Fryup. Mostly wide singletrack, this is best ridden when dry, as it gets very soft in wet weather and it gets more interesting as it becomes rockier on the far side. A long downhill on firm track along Glaisdale Rigg leads us into the village and a ford over the River Esk. We follow the lane to Lealholm Side and the gravel track over Lealholm Moor to Danby Beacon. We finish with a steep tarmac drop back to the car park, but don't forget that there is a junction at the bottom. This *is* squeaky brake time!

DANBY & GLAISDALE CIRCUIT

GRADE: ▲

TOTAL DISTANCE: 27.1KM » **TOTAL ASCENT:** 693M » **START GRID REFERENCE:** NZ 717084 » **SATNAV:** YO21 2NB
START/FINISH: DANBY LODGE CAR PARK » **PARKING:** DANBY LODGE CAR PARK (PAY AND DISPLAY)
CAFÉ: THE MOORS TEAROOM, DANBY LODGE TEL: 01287 660 362; STONEHOUSE BAKERY, DANBY TEL: 01287 660 006
PUBLIC HOUSE: DUKE OF WELLINGTON, DANBY TEL: 01287 660 351

© CROWN COPYRIGHT AND/OR DATABASE RIGHT. ALL RIGHTS RESERVED. LICENCE NUMBER 100

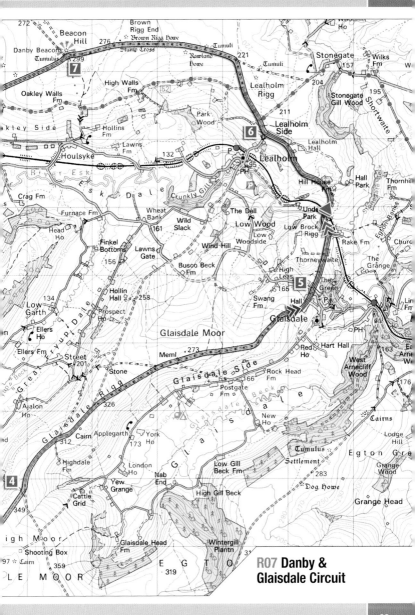

R07 Danby & Glaisdale Circuit

Directions – Danby & Glaisdale Circuit

⑤ Turn **R** out of the car park and follow the road into Danby village. At the crossroads turn **L**. Cross the bridge into Ainthorpe and turn left up lane signposted *Fryup*.

② Ignore first bridleway on right after the village and pass the tennis courts taking the next bridleway on the right at the road bend. Multiple tracks lead to a gate. **SA** at gate and follow the eroded track over Ainthorpe Rigg. 1km after the gate keep **SA** and follow the track down descent, technical at first with easy run-out to the road.

③ Turn **R** at the road signposted *Rosedale* and stay on the road for 4km. Turn **L** onto bridleway through gate signposted *Glaisdale 6 miles*. Follow the bridleway past Trough House and eventually onto rocky singletrack around the head of Fryup joining the Glaisdale/Rosedale road at the other side.

④ Turn **L** onto the road for 1.6km. At left bend go **SA** onto wide firm bridleway signposted *Glaisdale 2 miles*. Stay on this track for 4km to double gate and then 0.5km tarmac lane into Glaisdale.

⑤ Go **SA** at crossroads down lane for 500m. As lane turns right, go **SA** down doubletrack to ford signposted *Lealholm*. Bridge to left if river is too high to cross. Turn **L** after the ford on doubletrack bending right onto broken tarmac track over railway bridge and up a steep climb to farm. After the farm stay on tarmac lane to the road junction at Lealholm Side.

⑥ Turn **R** at the junction for 150m and then **L** at next junction signposted *Oakley Walls*. After 500m when road bends left go **SA** onto wide stony bridleway. After 400m turn **L** at the junction. Follow this track for 2.6km to the road at Danby Beacon.

⑦ Turn **L** onto the road signposted *Danby 1 mile*. Turn **L** at the bottom of the hill to return to the car park.

08 Hutton-le-Hole & Farndale

Introduction

This is an easy route to navigate. We start from one of the most picturesque villages on the moors and take in a delightful singletrack descent into Farndale with an easy tarmac finish on country lanes. To get the most out of the singletrack down into Farndale be sure to ride when the tracks are dry.

Route 14, Hutton-le-Hole, Farndale and Rosedale on page 83 is an extension to this ride if you fancy a bit more.

The Ride

We leave the village heading south and drop to the little known Dowthwaite Dale, with its wide, fast ford. After climbing out of the dale, an easy section of bridleway riding leads us to Gillamoor. There is a section of pleasant bridleway before a short tarmac workout brings us to the start of the long haul up Rudland Rigg. We turn off the Rigg onto a superb stretch of singletrack, riding the contours before dropping into the valley. This was the reason for the climb up Rudland Rigg, so lets make the most of it! More bridleway leads us on to Low Mill. We finish the ride on country lanes, enjoying the views of Farndale and a swift freewheel back to Hutton-le-Hole.

ALTITUDE PROFILE

HUTTON-LE-HOLE & FARNDALE   **GRADE:** ▲

TOTAL DISTANCE: 26.6KM » **TOTAL ASCENT:** 596M » **START GRID REFERENCE:** SE 704901 » **SATNAV:** YO62 6UA

START/FINISH: HUTTON-LE-HOLE » **PARKING:** HUTTON-LE-HOLE CAR PARK » **CAFÉ:** FORGE TEA SHOP, HUTTON-LE-HOLE

TEL: 01751 417444 » **PUBLIC HOUSE:** THE LION INN, BLAKEY RIDGE **TEL:** 01751 417320

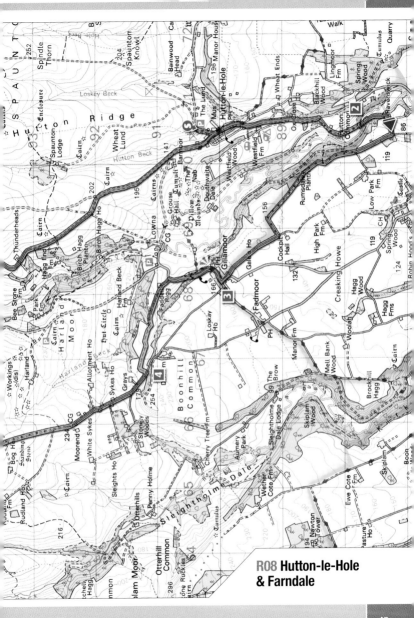

R08 Hutton-le-Hole & Farndale

Directions – Hutton-le-Hole & Farndale

↱ Turn **L** out of car park and **L** at the junction. Follow the road south through the village for 1.75km. Turn **R** onto narrow rough tarmac lane signposted *Dowthwaite Dale*. Follow this lane down to the ford.

2 Cross the ford by the footbridge and stay on the lane up a steep climb, past some farm buildings and to a T-junction. Turn **R** signposted *Low Park and High Park*. When the tarmac road bends left, go **SA** on to stony track. Stay on this track with the woods to the right, ignoring a track and a bridleway to the right. As the track meets a small forest on the left, ignore the track to right and stay **SA**. The track becomes gravel. Follow the track at a left bend to the lane at the end. Turn **R** to Gillamoor.

3 Turn **R** in Gillamoor, and **R** again towards the church. Follow the road as it bends left and down a hill. At the bottom, as the road bends right, turn **L** onto a bridleway, signposted to *Faddell Herd*. The bridleway is concreted up a steep hill to the farm at the top. Turn **L** and **SA** through a gate, onto soft but rideable doubletrack. Don't be put off by the yellow *Footpath* sign on the shed, this *is* a bridleway. With a fence on left go **SA** at two gates and 1.5km after the farm, turn **L** at two gates and follow the bridleway up a short hill to the road.

4 Turn **R** onto the road for almost 2km to a point where the road turns sharp left. Turn off the road and go **SA** onto a firm wide track with a blue *Unsuitable for Motors* sign. Stay on this track for 4.5km and a long climb up Rudland Rigg. Look out for the trig point on the left. 1km after the trig point, the track drops into a dip. In the dip the track is crossed by a bridleway.

5 Turn **R** onto doubletrack which turns sharp right after 20m. This track gradually turns to singletrack. Keep right at the cairn by a gully, and then after almost 1km turn **L** at the wooden *Bridleway* sign. Drop down over a small area of erosion to the gate. Go through the gate and turn **R** down to the wooded footbridge. Cross the bridge and go **SA** through the gates, following an often-muddy track over farmland to the Farndale road.

6 Turn **R** at the road, **L** in Low Mill and **R** at the next T-junction. Stay on this road all the way to the main Blakey road. Turn **R** to Hutton-le-Hole and then **L** as you enter the village to return to the car park.

09 Sneck Yate Bank

22.5km

Introduction

This is one for riders of all abilities, and includes a number of possible 'bail out' opportunities. Once the initial road work is over it's nearly all off-road with singletracks, forest roads, firm moor riding and one of the top ten downhills on the moors.

The Ride

A long, steady road section towards Sutton Bank gets our muscles warmed up but then it's nearly all off-road. Turning north onto the escarpment, an enjoyable singletrack weaves its way along the edge before turning off for the start of a fabulous downhill. We begin the descent passing under a larch-lined tunnel, then over short, rocky gardens and drop down into the quaint village of Boltby. From here the last, brief section of road climbs the lower slopes of Sneck Yate Bank, then turns into Boltby Forest for some easy forestry road riding past the reservoir. A stiff climb soon leads us onto more singletrack, climbing above Clarke Scars onto the old drover's road before a speedy descent towards Hawnby. Turn off before the quarry onto pleasant moorland tracks over Dale Town Common, finishing on a rocky road back to the car park.

ALTITUDE PROFILE

SNECK YATE BANK GRADE: ▲

TOTAL DISTANCE: 22.5KM » **TOTAL ASCENT:** 471M » **START GRID REFERENCE:** SE 509876
SATNAV: BOLTBY (CLOSEST) » **START/FINISH:** SNECK YATE BANK TOP » **PARKING:** SNECK YATE BANK TOP
CAFÉ: SUTTON BANK VISITOR CENTRE TEL: 01845 597426
PUBLIC HOUSE: THE WHITESTONECLIFFE INN, SUTTON-UNDER-WHITESTONECLIFFE TEL: 01845 597271

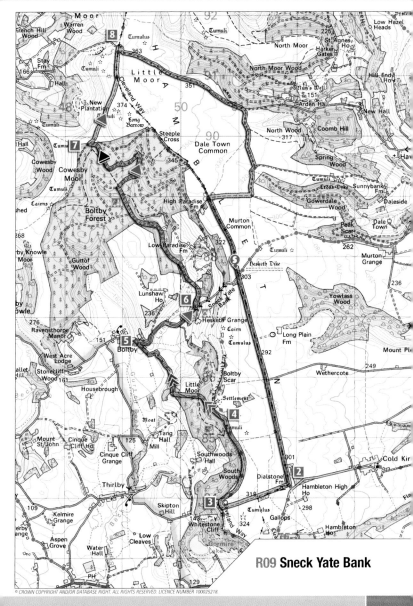

R09 Sneck Yate Bank

Directions – Sneck Yate Bank

➊ From the car park, head south onto a long straight lane towards Sutton Bank. Follow this lane for 3.5km to Dialstone Farm, just before the road junction.

2 Turn **R** immediately after the farm (the *Bridleway* sign is under a tree) onto a double farm track. (This track gets very sticky after rain!) After 400m turn **R** at a wall, through a gate and then **L** keeping copse of trees and wall to left. Another 800m brings you to another wall. Turn **R** with the track and follow it for 50m to a gate.

3 After the gate turn **R** onto fine singletrack along the escarpment. Stay with this along a long left curve for 1.7km to a point almost at the top of a rise and a *Bridleway* sign. Turn **L** here onto singletrack towards a gate into the woods after 80m.

4 Go through gate onto wide, larch-covered track angling down the forest. After left bend and short drop cross lane **SA** and then after 100m **SA** at single gate. Follow track down field towards trees. After gate turn immediately **R** and keep wall on left, signposted *Boltby*. **SA** at next couple of gates onto stony track, over ford and follow lane to Boltby village.

5 Turn **R** at Boltby and stay on the road for 1.4km climbing the lower part of Sneck Yate Bank. Turn **L** at the forest gate marked with a *Public Footpath* signpost. Don't be put off by this. To the left a poster welcomes all including cyclists to ride all tracks and paths in the forest!

6 Follow the track down a dip, over stream, ignoring track to left and pass reservoir to right. After a short climb turn **R** at junction and take the **L** turn after 350m. (This is the second major left on this forest road). Climb a steep, straight bank for 370m turning **L** at the top. The track becomes grassy singletrack. Follow to the next junction, turn **R** up singletrack marked with post and white sign. Follow this up a climb turning **L** at the top and up another steep climb to doubletrack bridleway and open moor.

7 Turn **R** for 50m to bridleway post and then **L** for 50m to moor gate. **SA** at gate and follow doubletrack climbing steeply at an angle. At the top keep **SA** with fence on left as far as the wall corner, turning right to gate. Go through gate and turn **L** onto wide track. Follow downhill for 500m turning **R** onto firm track.

8 Stay on this track for 2.5km. Just as the track begins to drop steeply after joining the wall on left for 200m, turn **R** on a sharp climb bending right. Follow over the hill dropping into a shallow valley with gate. Climb hill swinging right and then keep **R** at fork dropping into another shallow ravine. Keep to track over moor heading south for 500m taking a **R** fork over to a wall. Turn **R** at the wall and follow to next gate at 750m. Go through gate and turn **L** onto firm track and follow back to car park.

Introduction

A route with mostly firm, doubletrack riding, finishing with 3km of classic singletrack. Bransdale must be one of the quietest dales on the moors. The scenery is stunning and the ride into the dale from Rudland Rigg is long, fast and easy.

The Ride

We leave the car park and go straight into the climb onto Carr Ridge with some **G.O.A.P.** (**G**et **O**ff **A**nd **P**ush) before the easier riding on the ridge. (It's tough, but let's not forget that we'll be riding down here at the end!) We pass the highest point on the moors at Botton Head before the

fast descent to the old railway line. A short spurt along a stretch of singletrack and the railway trail leads us on to the rocky track over Rudland Rigg. Turn right at the track, crossing from Farndale to Bransdale and enjoy a long descent into the moors' quietest valley. A little more downhill on farm track takes us to Bransdale Mill. Follow a pleasant singletrack over the meadows, crossing the valley to Colt House Farm and the road on the west side of the valley. A couple of stiff climbs are followed by a welcome respite as the track heads north over Bransdale Ridge. We turn left at Stump Cross and the relish the wild descent into Tripsdale. Some easy riding at the top and great views of Hasty Bank lead us to the singletrack around Urra Moor. We need to take care crossing the stream before one last climb leads us back to the start of the great, rocky descent back down to Clay Bank.

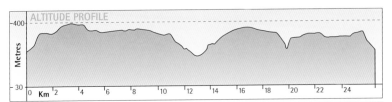

CLAY BANK & BRANSDALE　　　　　　　　　**GRADE:** ▲

TOTAL DISTANCE: 28.5KM **» TOTAL ASCENT:** 708M **» START GRID REFERENCE:** NZ 572035 **» SATNAV:** GT BROUGHTON
START/FINISH: CLAY BANK **» PARKING:** CLAY BANK CAR PARK **» CAFÉ:** SEVERAL IN STOKESLEY
PUBLIC HOUSE: THE BAY HORSE, GT BROUGHTON TEL: 01642 712319; THE BUCK INN, CHOP GATE TEL: 01642 778334

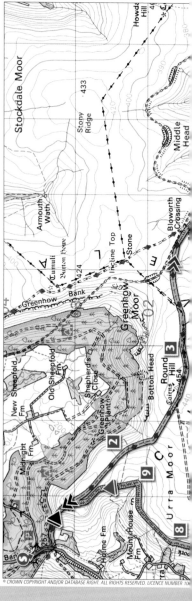

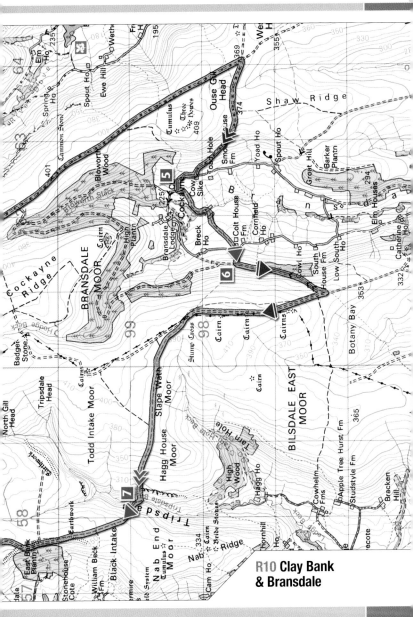

R10 Clay Bank & Bransdale

Directions – Clay Bank & Bransdale

↪ Turn **L** out of car park onto main road (not steep downhill). After 100m turn **L** at single gate onto rock stepped track. **SA** at single gate after 350m. Continue uphill keeping left at bottom of gully and near to the wall. Keep **SA** at single gate above gully.

2 Keep to wide singletrack past stone pillar on left and cairn on right. Pass bridleway to left. 300m after bridleway keep left at bend onto wide sandstone track. Keep **SA** after 600m with track from right. Pass trig point on left after 250m.

3 Keep **SA** downhill to sharp left bend. Go **SA** onto singletrack for 200m turning **R** onto old railway.

4 Turn **R** after 400m at Bloworth Crossing onto firm wide track. Follow this track for 4.7km to crossroads after slight descent (metal post on left). Turn **R** and follow across moor and after right bend downhill to the road in Bransdale.

5 Turn **R** on road to first left bend and then at the next right bend turn **L** onto firm track signposted *Bransdale Base Camp*. Follow this track to Bransdale Mill. Turn **R** after first building, cross over bridge and pass between two buildings to gate. **SA** at gate onto single grassy track with wall to right passing sundial on left. At wall corner head left across the field to the opposite wall corner marked with a standing stone. Ride between wall and ditch to single gate. Cross next field to double gate. Following wall on left pass farm buildings and at wall corner cross over to the double gate. Cross the lane and go **SA** at gate with *Bridleway* sign onto steep doubletrack leading up hill. At top of hill **SA** at gate, cross boggy patch and turn **L** onto the road.

6 Follow the road uphill past forest on left. Just at the very top, where the road bends left, turn **R** onto wide track bridleway. Look for a wooden signpost and a plaque (*Newton Tower Estate*). Follow this firm sandstone track for 2km to a fork 100m after a stone pillar on left at short drop. Follow doubletrack for 2.5km over Slape Wath Moor and a steep drop into Tripsdale.

7 Cross stream onto a steep, zig-zag climb leading to the top of hill overlooking Bilsdale. Turn **R** at T-junction, still on wide track. After 300m keep left with a bend to the right. Follow track through for 1.6km to T-junction. (Ignore singletrack in front by stone pillar). Turn **L** onto rough singletrack for 250m to a grassy bend. Turn **R** at small cairn onto singletrack. Follow with ditch to left leading to wall on left.

8 After 500m alongside the wall keep **SA** from wall corner bending right after 100m. Cross steep gully (bridleway post in gully). Continue on track around bend for 700m leading to drop to stream.

Danger! Keep right to avoid steep drop above stream.

9 Turn **L** after crossing steam and follow singletrack uphill for 1km running alongside earthworks to the gate at the top. Follow steep, paved track back down the right-hand side of the gully, keeping the wall to the right, to gate at bottom. Turn **R** on road to return to car park.

SECTION 3

Enduros

Warmed up? Enduros are rides that make the most of a day out in the hills. Make sure you've got your multi-tool, some lunch and some willing legs. These are challenging rides for fit, experienced riders who want to feel the burn.

Enduros
sponsored by

www.ibiscycles.com

11 Rosedale Abbey Circuit

25.3km

Introduction

Taking in one of the most talked about singletracks in the country (this is the singletrack that so many good things have been written about), this ride offers a mix of moors trail riding, shoulder-height bracken and forest track. Although the route finishes on road, don't be disappointed. The views from the cross at the top of Rosedale Bank are well worth a few minutes stop and contemplation before plunging into the final downhill – an exhilarating, brake-squealing finish.

The Ride

We start with a niggling worry that we are going to climb Chimney Bank, then breathe a sigh of relief as we turn off at the White Horse Farm Inn onto farm road leading to singletrack. 6km of glorious riding through the bracken leads us to a little road work and a climb to the village of Cropton, complete with its own brewery at The New Inn, for those of us in need of refreshment. A little more tarmac follows, before thrusting deep into Cropton Forest on good forest road. We take a brief singletrack interlude in the middle and then continue to the forest edge, picking up a not-so-well-known stretch of great singletrack. A tough section of riding and navigating takes us over Hamer Moor onto moorland track leading to the road for Rosedale.

ALTITUDE PROFILE

ROSEDALE ABBEY CIRCUIT **GRADE:** ▲

TOTAL DISTANCE: 25.3KM » TOTAL ASCENT: 592M » START GRID REFERENCE: SE 724959 » SATNAV: YO18 8RA
START/FINISH: ROSEDALE ABBEY » PARKING: EITHER SIDE OF THE MILLBURN ARMS » CAFÉ: ABBEY TEAROOM AND STORE TEL: 01751 417475, MOLLY'S FARM SHOP AND TEAROOM TEL: 01751 417 468 – BOTH ROSEDALE ABBEY
PUBLIC HOUSE: THE MILLBURN ARMS, ROSEDALE ABBEY TEL: 01751 417312; THE NEW INN, CROPTON TEL: 01751 417330

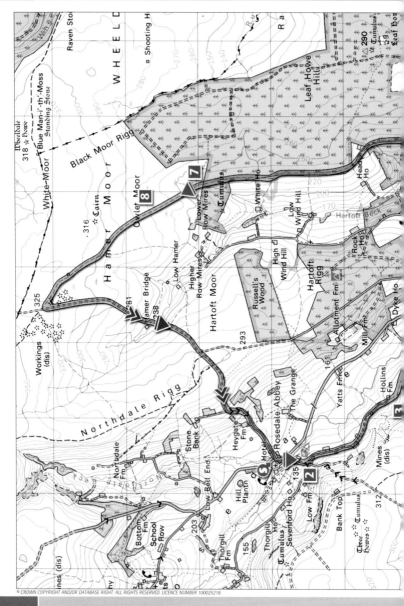

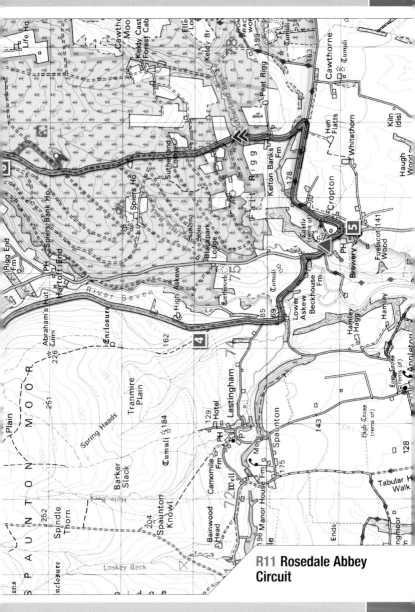

R11 Rosedale Abbey Circuit

Directions – Rosedale Abbey Circuit

❻ Turn **L** out of the car park for 150m and then **R** onto the Chimney Bank Road, signposted *Hutton-le-Hole*. Climb the hill for 300m to the White Horse Farm Inn, turning **L** into the car park.

2 Go straight through the car park picking up a firm track at the far side. Pass house on right, **SA** at gate. Follow down bend, over cattle grid to gate. 100m after gate turn **R** at *Bridleway* sign before farm up a grass bank to wall corner on left.

3 Keep left with the wall ignoring track forking right. At 200m take either fork. At next wall corner track forks, keep right with bridleway post. Track turns to singletrack over rocks swinging right under trees. Follow the track with diversions for 2.2km to wall corner.

4 Keep to wide track right of wall for another 500m joining farm road. Turn **R** and follow up hill and then down to road. Turn **L** at road and follow round left bend and onto bridge leading to the Rosedale road. Turn **R** and climb hill into Cropton.

5 Turn **L** in Cropton and follow the road for 1.5km. 50m after passing the lane end to Hen Flatts on right, turn **L** into lane ('James Cameron' iron bench on corner). Follow lane downhill and **SA** at junction near Kelton Banks Farm. Continue downhill, and cross the ford onto forest road. Stay **SA** on this road for 2.5km to T-junction*. Go **SA** onto singletrack at *Bridleway* sign for 800m to forest road corner.

> ◤OR▷ **Alternative to singletrack:* Turn **R** at T-junction uphill for 650m. Turn first **L** down to join at forest road corner.

6 From bridleway go **SA** onto forest road – *or **R** if joining from ◤OR▷ – and follow for 1.2km to gate at St James Farm. **SA** at gate onto farm track and **SA** at next two gates. Follow rough doubletrack through woods for 350m joining fence on left and singletrack. Keep fence to left for 650m turn **L** at gate and turn immediately **R** before the *Bridleway* sign following grass track with fence to right. (This 'detour' off the singletrack is to keep with the legal right of way). Follow this for 250m and pass through single gate back onto singletrack with fence to left. After 400m track goes into forest briefly winding in and out of trees leading onto the main forest road after 300m.

7 Go **SA** over the road onto singletrack with wall on left for 20m to single gate. Cross stream onto singletrack. Track turns left away from stream after 50m and eventually becomes indistinct over a wide grassy area. Aim North West for 150m picking out a 2-feet-tall standing stone which marks a singletrack. Follow this track for 300m joining a shallow gully. Cross gully to far side and follow the line of gully over the crest of the hill dropping down on doubletrack to gate.

8 **SA** at gate onto rutted track over moor for 1km to wall corner. Pick up a sandstone track from the left with wall to right for 500m and then cross moor to road. Turn **L** at road and follow down dip over Hamer Beck and short climb before dropping back into Rosedale Abbey.

12 Blakey Bank Circuit

33.3km

Introduction

If you start high you finish high! This route is certainly no exception to that rule. The start spoils you with two short sections of sweet singletrack and then a sweeping singletrack downhill into Westerdale. The rest of the route is a mixture of hard work on short but steep climbs and fantastic moors scenery, culminating in the gruelling climb out of Farndale up Blakey Bank.

The Ride

We leave the car park and head up the hill past The Lion Inn to the first section of singletrack, which weaves across the head of Rosedale. Crossing the road at White Cross, we have more singletrack before the downhill into Dale Head in Westerdale. The first climb starts on the road out of Westerdale. The ford at Hob Hole puts an end to any chance of a 'run in' before we tackle the almost vertical climb to the Baysdale bridleway. The rocky journey into Baysdale is wonderful and we shall soon be hacking through the bracken before a bouncing drop to the valley floor. A section of easy riding follows before the long climb up the western spur of Grains Beck and the 1km-long straight to Burton Howe. With terrific views towards the Cleveland Hills we enjoy a spell of easy riding as we turn onto the old railway at Bloworth Crossing. Another fantastic downhill to Farndale prepares us for that last promised climb to the finish. Alternatively, stay on the railway all the way back to the top of Blakey Bank.

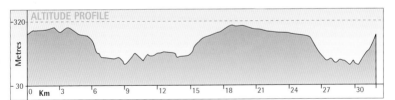

ALTITUDE PROFILE

Metres — 320, 30

Km: 0, 3, 6, 9, 12, 15, 18, 21, 24, 27, 30

BLAKEY BANK CIRCUIT — **GRADE:** ▲

TOTAL DISTANCE: 33.3KM » **TOTAL ASCENT:** 883M » **START GRID REFERENCE:** SE 683989

SATNAV: YO62 7LQ (LION INN) » **START/FINISH:** TOP OF BLAKEY BANK, BLAKEY RIDGE » **PARKING:** TOP OF BLAKEY BANK OR AT THE LION INN » **CAFÉ:** FORGE TEA SHOP, HUTTON-LE-HOLE TEL: 01751 417444 » **PUBLIC HOUSE:** THE LION INN, BLAKEY RIDGE TEL: 01751 417320; THE FEVERSHAM ARMS, CHURCH HOUSES TEL: 01751 433206

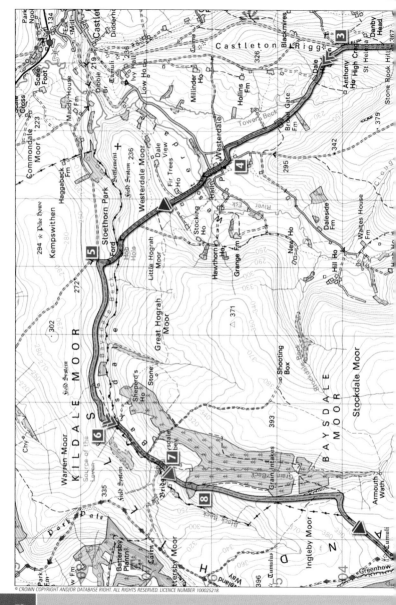

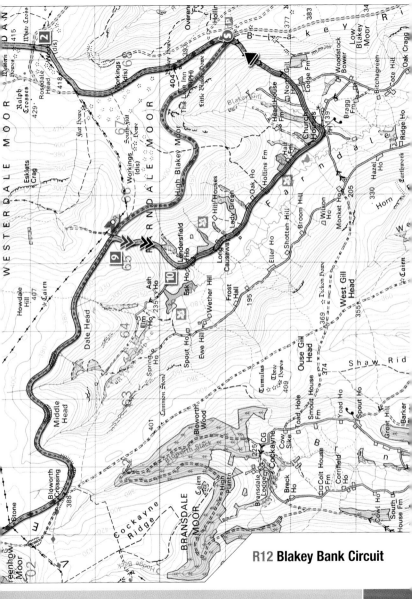

R12 Blakey Bank Circuit

Directions – Blakey Bank Circuit

↪ Turn **R** out of car park and pass The Lion Inn on your left. Approx. 1.5km after the Inn look out for a wide standing stone at the start of a track on the left. Turn **R** just opposite onto singletrack marked with a wooden post.

2 After about 1.5km cross the road **SA** onto another singletrack passing White Cross to the left. Follow this for 1km to the road. Turn **R** heading north for another 1km to the next bridleway on the left just opposite a lane dropping sharply on the right.

3 Turn **L** onto the bridleway down to Dale Head Farm. Pass through the gate and turn **L** at tree and sign and pass between two buildings. Turn **R**, pass farmhouse and take right fork to gate at corner of wall. **SA** at gate and after 100m go between wall and hedge. **SA** with wall on left for 150m to sharp **R** at the bottom of field. Follow track with stream on left for 30m turning **L** over bridge to gate. Climb **SA** to gate and **SA** again with wall to left. 100m and **SA** at gate with wall on right and **SA** at farm gates onto farm lane. 700m after the farm turn **L** at the junction and then **R** into Westerdale.

4 Go down through the village, climb over Westerdale Moor and drop down to the ford in Hob Hole. Stay with the road for a very steep climb away from the ford for 400m to a bridleway on the left opposite a lane.

5 Turn **L** onto a rocky doubletrack. Stay with the track for almost 2km to a barn. Ignore the bridleway climbing to the right and go **SA** towards the wall crossing a stream at a wooden post with a white and yellow marker. Edge along the right-hand side of the wall. Stay with the wall as it bends to left and then at the point of two trees turn **R** and cross 50m of bog to the wall at the forest edge. Turn **R** at this wall and stay with the wall for 300m to the wall corner and single gate to **L**.

6 Turn **L** through the gate and drop down between to rows of gorse to a farm building. The track swings to the right here to a wide cattle bridge at the bottom. Cross the bridge turning **R** and then **SA** at the gate onto a firm farm lane. Take this lane all the way to Baysdale Abbey.

7 As the lane bends to the right at the Abbey go **SA** over a wide verge to two gates. Go **SA** at the left gate into a wide pasture. Cut across the field passing trees and aiming for a dip in the wall ahead at the top of a climb on the edge of a forest. Pass through the gate and take the right fork and follow a muddy track bending sharply first to the left and then right through the forest to another gate leading to the moor.

8 Go **SA** at the gate and follow a firm track for 2km and turn sharp **R** and climb a sandstone track for 2km all the way to Burton Howe. Go past the 'Howe' and turn **L** onto firm doubletrack. Follow this track for almost 2km to Bloworth Crossing. Turn **L** onto the old railway. After 5km the track opens up on a high embankment. Half way along the embankment a track crosses from The Esklets to Farndale with a signpost on the left.

9 Turn **R** down a raised track crossing a shallow gully after 300m and on to a gate. **SA** at gate keeping to left of the gully for another 200m to the next gate where the stream disappears underneath. Go through the gate onto a wide excavated track with a deeper ravine to the left. The track turns grassy to the next gate at the wall. Go **SA** keeping to the left of shallow gully using the tree in front as a guide. Turn **R** over a stone shelf bridge crossing the gully and then **L** with the wall on the left to the gate at the bottom.

> *Alternatively, continue **SA** at The Esklets/Farndale junction to return to the start along the old railway.

10 Turn **L** at the lane for a swift ride to Church Houses. Turn **L** at the Feversham Arms and the **L** again to begin the climb up Blakey Bank. Cross the road at the top to finish at the car park.

13 Black Hambleton & Hawnby 30.6km

Introduction

This superb route follows some well-known moorland tracks, particularly the Drover's Road, with its panoramic views to the west. To mix things up, there is also a little-known moorland singletrack sweeping down from Cock Howe with a few hidden 'surprise' drop-offs. More singletrack on Locker Low Moor helps keep tired legs going to the finish.

The Ride

No messing about here! This route takes us straight into an off-road climb on Black Hambleton. Mostly do-able but a little rocky section near the top may beat a few of us. Cruise down the Drover's Road and then into top gear to fly down the old quarry road by Arden Hall. A fine bridleway provides an alternative to the road around Coomb Hill and gives us a moment of peaceful tranquillity at Stoney Gill Hole. A little road work brings us to the Hawnby Post Office Tea Room (tea and buns, anyone?) and then around Hawnby Hill Crag. Typical moors track leads the way directly to the Bilsdale Mast and Cock Howe before turning onto 1.5km of singletrack, technical in parts, weaving and dipping in the heather. This route finishes with another shorter stretch of singletrack on Locker Low Moor – a delight to ride when dry but a nightmare when it's wet!

ALTITUDE PROFILE

Metres

BLACK HAMBLETON & HAWNBY — **GRADE:** ▲

TOTAL DISTANCE: 30.6KM **»** **TOTAL ASCENT:** 718M **»** **START GRID REFERENCE:** SE 479959
SATNAV: OSMOTHERLEY (CLOSEST) **»** **START/FINISH:** SQUARE CORNER CAR PARK ABOVE OSMOTHERLEY
PARKING: SQUARE CORNER CAR PARK **»** **CAFÉ:** HAWNBY POST OFFICE TEAROOM TEL: 01439 798223; CHEQUERS TEAROOM
TEL: 01609 883710, EAST OF OSMOTHERLEY **»** **PUBLIC HOUSE:** QUEEN CATHERINE HOTEL TEL: 01609 883209, THE GOLDEN
LION TEL: 01609 883526, BOTH OSMOTHERLEY; THE INN AT HAWNBY, TEL: 01439 798202

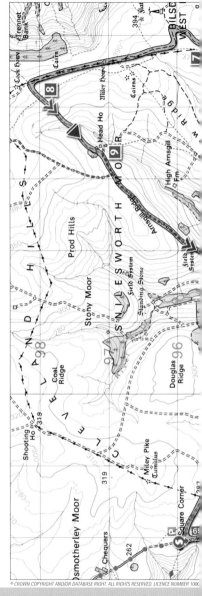

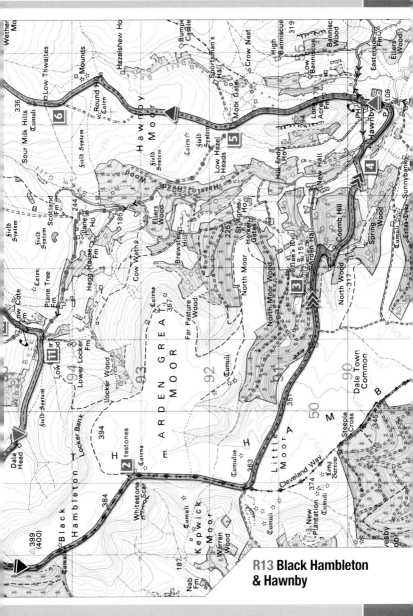

R13 Black Hambleton & Hawnby

Directions – Black Hambleton & Hawnby

➎ Take the firm bridleway south from the car park towards Black Hambleton. After 300m go **SA** at a gate and the track begins the climb on Black Hambleton. Stay on this firm doubletrack bridleway with a wall on the right, blocking most of the view, as far as White Gill Head, the first track junction.

2 Take the track to the right and cross a cattle grid gate onto the wide Drover's Road. Keep to this wide expanse of track, **SA** at a gate and up to the next crossroads. Take the track **L**, opposite the gate and information board, follow it **SA** at two further gates and past the old quarry on the right. This is a fast descent and you need to look out for the gate halfway down which is easy to miss!

3 As you pass the lane into Arden Hall the track turns to road. Continue for 370m. As the road bends left turn **R** up an often-muddy track bridleway. After 200m go **SA** at the gate under the tree and keep the fence to the right crossing a field for 80m to join a firmer track coming from the gate to the right. Turn **L** onto this track and keep **L** at the next fork and follow through to the next two gates with fence on right and follow down through the pasture to gate near a stone bridge.

4 Turn **R** onto the road and follow for 300m taking the next **R**. Follow into the lower part of Hawnby, past the tea room, and take the next **L** for a stiff climb to a T-junction at the top of the hill. Turn **R** at the junction and follow the road around a left bend heading north, ignoring the turn off to the right bend. Stay on this road heading north until the next cattle grid, almost 2km further on.

5 Over the cattle grid there is a wide parking area on the right. Take the first wide track to the **L** with blue sign *Unsuitable for Motor Vehicles* (the Bilsdale mast is straight ahead). Follow this for 1.2km and fork **R** at a *Bridleway* sign. Fence then wall on right. 50m after the wall turns away take a **L** fork and **L** again at the next fork towards a stone wall. At the wall turn **L** and climb a gentle hill with the wall on the right to rejoin the main track at a *Bridleway* sign.

6 Turn **R** onto the track and continue with the wall on right. Stay with this track as it continues towards the mast, mingling briefly with the footpath. A few turns bring you to a track junction almost under the mast.

7   Turn **L** here onto a rough track, mostly long grass and heather but still rideable. After 250m the track turns sharp **R**. Follow for another 850m to another track junction. Turn **R** onto a sandstone track and stay with this for almost 1.5km to Cock Howe. As the track turns past Cock Howe, look out for a singletrack to the **L**. It is marked by a small pile of stones and a pole (which is usually lying on the heather).

8   Take this track and follow it for 900m to a stream crossing. Watch out for the hidden drop offs! Cross the stream and stay with the singletrack, climbing up the other side and then crossing over a grassy area to a wall corner. Continue with the wall on the left and on past the small woods to the right and join a wider track leading out of farmland to the left.

9   Turn **R** and take this track all the way along Arnsgill Ridge and down through two gates to a narrow lane at Hill End Farm. Turn **R** on the lane and down to a gate onto another concreted lane. Turn **L** and follow down over a cattle grid on to Low Cote Farm at the road bend.

10   From here go **SA** down the road. At the bottom of the hill turn right over a stream and **SA** to gate with a sign for *Lower Locker Farm*. After the gate the farm track bends **L** and after the bend you will see a bridleway post on the **R**. Turn **R** here through a single gate and up a grassy field with the fence on the left to another gate leading to the moor.

11   This singletrack is easy to follow heading straight for the old farm buildings at Dale Head. If visibility is good the buildings are always in view. As the track nears the buildings it drops to a small stream. Take the right fork before the drop. Cross the 'more than adequate' bridge and then climb up a grassy field clearly marked with *Bridleway* signs. Turn sharp **L** at the buildings and then **R** before the ruins. Continue on doubletrack through two gates. After 800m the track turns sharp **R**, crosses a stream and another gate leads to short climb to the road. Turn **L** at the road to return to the car park.

14 Hutton-le-Hole, Farndale & Rosedale

39.5km

Introduction

This route is an alternative longer version of Route 8, Hutton-le-Hole & Farndale on page 43, with some steady riding after a hard climb out of Farndale to Blakey Ridge. Enjoy the views into Rosedale from the old railway line followed by a potential 4km freewheel (with a tailwind) down to Lastingham.

The Ride

We leave the village heading south away from the moors and drop to the little-known Dowthwaite Dale, with its wide, fast ford. After a climb out of Dowthwaite an easy section of bridleway riding leads us to Gillamoor. A pleasant section of bridleway follows and after a short tarmac workout we reach the start of the long haul up Rudland Rigg. We turn off the Rigg onto a superb stretch of singletrack that traces the contours, before dropping into the valley. More bridleway leads on to Low Mill. The valley road climbs long and steeply up to Blakey Ridge. The hard work over with, its 6.5km of easy riding with wonderful views across and into Rosedale. The ride finishes on a long descent to Lastingham and a short stretch of road back to Hutton-le-Hole.

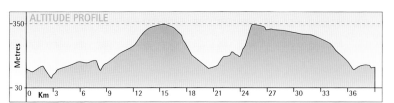

ALTITUDE PROFILE

Metres

0 Km 3 6 9 12 15 18 21 24 27 30 33 36

HUTTON-LE-HOLE, FARNDALE & ROSEDALE   GRADE: ▲

TOTAL DISTANCE: 39.5KM » **TOTAL ASCENT:** 876M » **START GRID REFERENCE:** SE 704901 » **SATNAV:** YO62 6UA
START/FINISH: HUTTON-LE-HOLE CAR PARK » **PARKING:** HUTTON-LE-HOLE » **CAFÉ:** FORGE TEA SHOP, HUTTON-LE-HOLE
TEL: 01751 417444; THE LASTINGHAM GRANGE HOTEL TEL: 01751 417 345 » **PUBLIC HOUSE:** THE LION INN, BLAKEY RIDGE
TEL: 01751 417320; THE BLACKSMITHS ARMS, LASTINGHAM TEL: 01751 417247

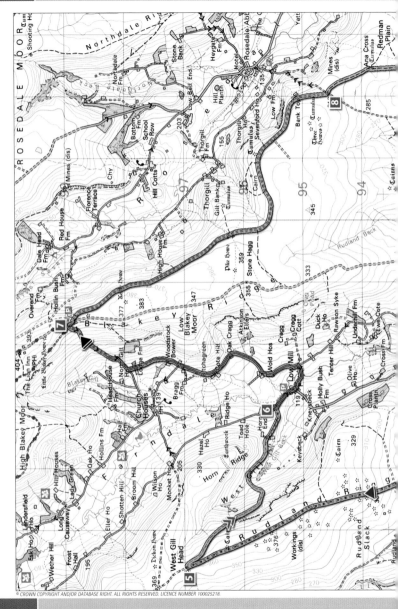

R14 Hutton-le-Hole, Farndale & Rosedale

Directions – Hutton-le-Hole, Farndale & Rosedale

➏ Turn **L** out of car park and **L** at junction. Follow the road **SA** through the village for 1.75km. Turn **R** onto narrow, rough tarmac lane signposted to *Dowthwaite Dale*. Follow this lane down to the ford.

2 Cross the ford by the footbridge and stay on the lane up a steep climb, past some farm buildings and to a T-junction. Turn **R**, signposted *Low Park and High Park*. Stay on this track with the woods to the right ignoring a track to the right and bridleway to the right. As the track meets a small forest on the left, ignore the track to right and stay **SA**, the track becoming gravelled. Follow the track at a left bend to the lane at the end. Turn **R** to Gillamoor.

3 Turn **R** at the junction in Gillamoor and follow the road as it bends left and down a hill. At the bottom as the road bends right turn **L** onto a bridleway signposted to *Faddell Herd*. The bridleway is concreted up a steep hill to the farm at the top. Turn **L** and **SA** through a gate onto soft but rideable doubletrack. Don't be put off by the yellow *Footpath* sign on the shed. This is a bridleway. With fence on left go **SA** at two gates and 1.5km after the farm turn **L** at two gates and follow the bridleway up a short hill to the road.

4 Turn **R** onto the road for almost 2km to point where the road turns sharp left. Turn off the road and go **SA** onto a firm wide track with a blue *Unsuitable for Motors* sign. Stay on this track for 4.5km and a long climb up Rudland Rigg. Look out for the trig point on the left. 1km after the trig point the track drops into a dip. In the dip the track is crossed by a bridleway.

5 Turn **R** onto doubletrack which turns sharp right after 20m. This track gradually turns to singletrack. Keep right at the cairn by a gully and then almost another 1km turn **L** at wooden *Bridleway* sign. Drop down over a small area of erosion to the gate. Go through the gate and turn **L** down to the wooded footbridge. Cross the bridge and go **SA** through the gates follow a muddy track over farmland to the Farndale road.

6 Turn **R** at the road and then **L** in Low Mill and **L** at the next T-junction. After 3.5km turn right at the next junction to begin the climb to Blakey Ridge.

7 Cross the road **SA** through an open parking area onto the old railway track. Turn **R** and follow this track for 6.5km to the road at the top of Chimney Bank.

8 Cross the road and go **SA** onto a wide track. Follow this track for 700m and turn **R** up a short singletrack to Ana Cross. Head **SA** at the cross onto wide track again for 550m to the next junction. Turn **R** and stay on this track down Lastingham ridge for 2km passing the stone on left and signpost on right just before the gate.

9 Go **SA** at the gate down a steep lane. Turn **R** at the bottom and **R** again at the Blacksmiths Arms pub. Keep **R** again at the next junction follow the lane for 2km back to the car park.

15 Rosedale & Fryup

34.4km

Introduction

Get ready for one of the best singletracks on the moors, followed by one of the most technical, demanding downhills. When that's all over, we can catch our breath in a tranquil setting with stunning scenery all around. If that's not enough, we get the best section of the old Rosedale railway to ride towards the end of the route.

The Ride

We leave Rosedale Abbey, heading north up the dale to Hill Cottages. Turning off here, we climb Sturdy Bank to the road at the top for a short ride on tarmac to the paved causeway and a few technical drop-offs over Glaisdale Moor. After appreciating the breathtaking views over Fryup Edge, we edge our way down a rocky descent into the basin below. If we're going to stop anywhere for a break this is the place for it! A fast section of singletrack through the dale leads to the road and a long tarmac climb up Danby High Moor. We take a singletrack shortcut across the head of Rosedale to the main road on Blakey Ridge. Turn left onto the old railway shortly after The Lion Inn and follow the railway around the head of the valley. This is the most interesting and testing part of the railway to ride, with sections of singletrack, a steep drop off, and a couple of technical water (or mud) splashes for us to cross. Then we turn off the railway for a short singletrack descent to Dale Head Farm, cross the valley floor on a narrow lane and pick up the bridleway before Moorlands Farm to ride south through the valley past Thorgill. We finish by turning onto Chimney Bank and dropping back into Rosedale Abbey.

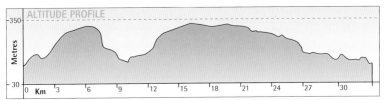

ALTITUDE PROFILE

Metres

350

30

0 Km 3   6   9   12   15   18   21   24   27   30

ROSEDALE & FRYUP

GRADE: ▲

TOTAL DISTANCE: 34.4KM **»** **TOTAL ASCENT:** 863M **»** **START GRID REFERENCE:** SE 724959 **»** **SATNAV:** YO18 8RA
START/FINISH: ROSEDALE ABBEY **»** **PARKING:** EITHER SIDE OF THE MILBURN ARMS **»** **CAFÉ:** ABBEY TEAROOM AND STORE TEL: 01751 417475, MOLLY'S FARM SHOP AND TEAROOM TEL: 01751 417468 – BOTH ROSEDALE ABBEY
PUBLIC HOUSE: THE MILLBURN ARMS, ROSEDALE ABBEY TEL: 01751 417312

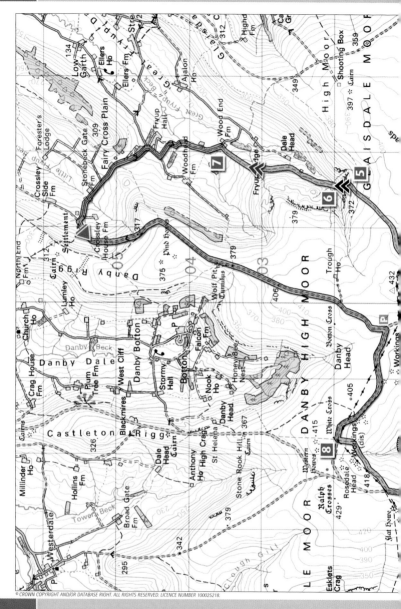

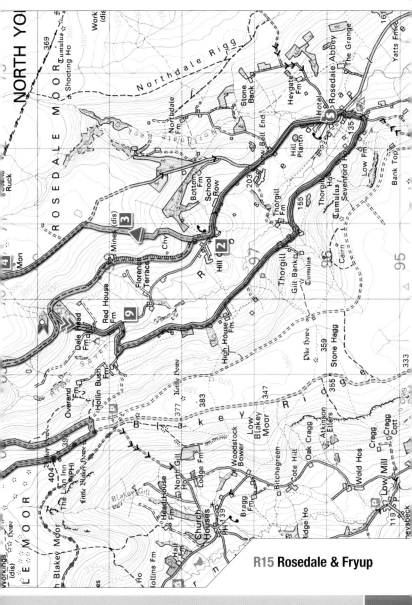

R15 **Rosedale & Fryup**

Directions – Rosedale & Fryup

1 Turn **R** out of car park and **R** at the T-junction. 300m after Bell End corner, turn off **L** onto road signposted *Daleside*. Keep to the road for a further 1km past a double row of cottages to the bridleway on the right just after the telephone box.

2 Turn **R** onto a firm track leading up the hill. Pass by the farm and turn **R** after the gate onto a doubletrack. Follow the track up the hill for 450m to the wall corner. At the corner the track swings away from the wall climbing for a further 400m to a fence corner on the right and sheep pen on the left.

3 At this point the bridleway swings off left but it is very difficult to follow and ride. It is better to stay on the defined track that becomes more firm leading to the road 200m south of the bend at Clough Dike Head. Turn **L** onto the road for 2km passing the bridleway on the left to a point where a bridleway is signposted on both sides of the road.

4 Turn **R** onto very narrow singletrack. It's like this for 150m before hitting the paved causeway. Follow the causeway for 1.5km and then more singletrack bending right over the moor. The last 100m is through long grass and can be boggy.

5 Turn **R** onto doubletrack and then after 50m and cairn turn **L** onto singletrack. Take care here. After less then 200m the track dips suddenly turning sharp **L** becoming very steep and rocky (Slippery when wet. Photo on page 88). Only the highly skilled will be able to ride this part of the downhill. At the last right-hand bend the track becomes rideable again (for the less skilled) dropping into the valley head.

6 Cross the stream to the left climbing singletrack to double gate. Pass through the gate and follow wide singletrack down the valley, alongside the wall. **SA** at all gates. After crossing the ford, the next gate leads into a field. Follow the track keeping the bushes to the left crossing at the next gate with fence on the right down to the road.

7 Turn **L** on the road. Follow the road up the hill to the next junction. Turn **L**, climbing over the ridge dropping into Little Fryup Dale. Turn **L** at the next junction shortly after Stonebeck Gate Farm. Follow the road up a stiff climb and then for another 2km after the top bend to another junction above Rosedale. Turn **R** for 1.7km to bridleway on both sides of road at White Cross.

8 Turn **L** onto singletrack bridleway across the head of Rosedale. Turn **L** at the other side onto road. Pass The Lion Inn on right and then turn **L** 500m after the inn onto firm doubletrack. Turn **L** after 100m onto old railway track. Follow this around the head of the valley to the east side. At the left bend before the large embankment a bridleway crosses the track down to Dale Head Farm. Turn **R** here onto singletrack keeping the wall on the right. Follow down to road and turn **L**.

During or after bad weather, continue along the railway to return to the start.

9 After 470m turn **R** down narrow lane. Turn **L** onto bridleway 150m before Moorlands Farm. After 50m keep wall to right and follow the wall around to gate. **SA** at all gates through to Thorgill joining a lane. Turn **L** at junction with Rosedale Bank and **L** after the bridge back into Rosedale Abbey.

16 Ravenscar – Big Country

Introduction

This is the 'Big Country' ride! The sea views are wonderful and the moorland views stretch for miles. Be ready for a pure cross-country route, with little in the way of white-knuckle downhills but instead a good mix of terrain and jaw-dropping scenery to keep it interesting. Choose a dry, clear day to get the best out of this route.

The Ride

Take a short tarmac warm-up to the mast on Beacon Howes before turning south on some great singletrack along Green Dike. Forest road leads over Pye Rigg and the busy A171 before fine riding through Harwood Dale forest. This leads into Harwood Dale before the long pull up to Lilla Cross. The eroded gullies take the mind off the grind and add a little fun to the climb. From the Louven Howe a wide track descends through Newton House Plantations to the tourist beauty spot at May Beck. Some necessary road riding leads back to the A171 before picking up the bridleway (sea views abound) and dropping down to the old railway and the return to Ravenscar.

RAVENSCAR – BIG COUNTRY   GRADE: ▲»▲

TOTAL DISTANCE: 36.7KM » **TOTAL ASCENT:** 702M » **START GRID REFERENCE:** NZ 980015 **SATNAV:** RAVENSCAR
START/FINISH: RAVENSCAR » **PARKING:** RAVENSCAR ROAD SIDE PARKING
CAFÉ: RAVENSCAR TEAROOMS TEL: 01723 870444

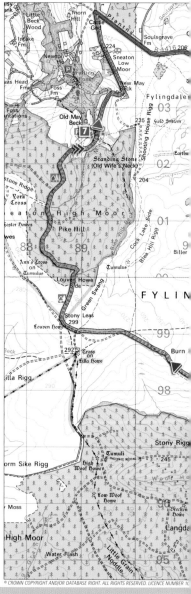

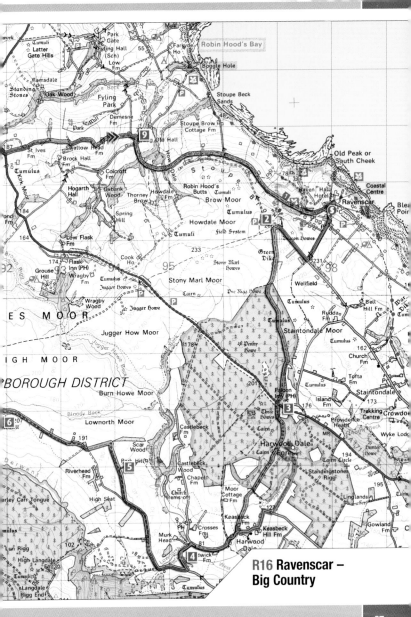

R16 Ravenscar – Big Country

Directions – Ravenscar – Big Country

↪ From roadside parking head south west away from Ravenscar back to the T-junction. Turn **R** towards the mast. At 800m (opposite the mast) turn **L** at wall corner and *Bridleway* sign onto singletrack.

2 Follow singletrack with wall to left for 1.1km to forest edge. Turn **R** at forest edge and then after 50m turn **L** into the forest on more singletrack. Singletrack becomes doubletrack after 1km. Shortly after track change follow around right bend and then after another 150m turn **L**. Follow doubletrack through to A171.

3 Cross road (take care very busy road) and go **SA** at gate onto forest road signed *Moors to Sea*. After 900m at junction go **SA** onto singletrack. Boggy in places but rideable. At 250m cross track keeping **SA**. Follow for 600m to wall. Turn **R** for 30m and then **L** through gate marked bridleway. Cross the field towards the beck bending left. Keep the stream to the right as track becomes indistinct. In the corner, cross the beck and go through the gate. **SA** on singletrack with stream and bushes to right. After 200m go **SA** at double gate with wall to left. **SA** at metal gate onto farm lane. Follow through to road and turn **R** to Harwood Dale village.

> **OR** **Misses out the boggy singletrack**
> Cross road (take care very busy road) and go **SA** at gate onto forest road signed *Moors to Sea*. After 900m at junction turn **L** on forest track and follow around the sharp right bend. After 140m from the bend turn **R** onto gravelled track and follow through to the road. Turn **R** towards Harwood Dale village.

4 700m after village turn **L** at T-junction and take next **R** uphill signposted *Low North Camp*. Follow this farm road for 1.1km to farm on the hill. Continue **SA** for another 800m. Shortly after climb on concrete track turn **R** onto farm track bridleway.

5 **SA** at gate on hill up to metal gate at top. Turn **L** before the gate onto grassy singletrack keeping fence to right. **SA** at single gate and then at next gate turn **R** onto farm track. Stay on this track becoming singletrack for 1.7km turning double to the moor gate.

6 Go **SA** onto sandstone doubletrack. At 2.3km turn **L** at junction. After 500m turn **R** at junction. (Continue **SA** for Lilla Cross and turn **R** after cross to rejoin route). At 700m keep **SA** at *Bridleway* sign. Turn **R** after another 300m at junction and **SA** at gate onto wide gravel track. Follow the track down into the forest, bending left after 250m and then right after another 800m. Follow for 900m, turning right leading to the car park at May Beck.

7 From May Beck follow the road up the bank past the caravan site to the B1416. Turn **R** at junction and **R** at next junction onto A171. (**Take care very busy road.**) There is enough space to ride on the grass verge if necessary. Drop down in the dip and climb for 400m to bridleway on left.

8 Turn **L** signposted *St Ives*. Follow the rough tarmac track down to St Ives Farm. Continue around the right of farm through gate and onto double grassy track. After 400m go **SA** at gate into woods. Keep right at signpost with fence to right. **SA** at gate out of woods into field with wall to right. Follow wall to right hand corner of field and turn **R** between walls. Go **SA** at gate and **L** at the next junction with wall to left. Follow through field cutting across to far left corner. Pick up a double deep rutted farm track leading to Swallow Head Farm. Keep **SA** at gate through farmyard and continue with bushes to left on tarmac farm road to road at bottom.

9 Turn **R** and after left bend turn **R** onto old railway. Follow the railway all the way back to Ravenscar.

Introduction

This is a classic XC moors route with plenty of typical moors track and some lovely singletrack riding. Fans of the ITV series Heartbeat will enjoy this ride even more. A section of forest roads provides variety, and if you're lucky, the sights and sounds of steam locomotives will add a touch of nostalgia. Best tackled during dry weather!

The Ride

We leave the village by road, crossing the bridge that overlooks the railway station. A steep climb leads on to a longer road climb, after which we switch onto bridleway that takes us over Sneaton High Moor. This section is fun and technical in the ruts when dry, but hard going when wet. Stay on this track all the way to Lilla Cross where the riding becomes more firm and faster on gravelled track. We can't linger too long here past Fylingdales lest we are investigated by patrolling police cars. Singletrack leads us to Malo Cross, from where an easy climb leads onto the wide escarpment of Saltersgate Brow and a vast panorama over the moors to the west. Singletrack bridleway leads us safely around the head of the 'Hole of Horcum' and onto doubletrack over Levisham Moor. Careful navigation brings us to a surprise downhill at Pillow Mounde, with a short tarmac downhill to Levisham station. Leave the whistles and steam behind and follow the forest road parallel with the railway to Raper's. A steep climb brings some great views into Newton Dale and singletrack to Rotten Gill and Blawath Beck. Not quite so Rotten from here, but 4km of blissful singletrack to the Tarn at Old Kit Bield, finishing with a short sweeping grassy downhill over Moss Rigg into Goathland.

ALTITUDE PROFILE

Metres

-300

-30

0 Km   3   6   9   12   15   18   21   24   27   30   33

GOATHLAND CIRCUIT

GRADE: ▲»▲

TOTAL DISTANCE: 36.7KM » **TOTAL ASCENT:** 693M » **START GRID REFERENCE:** NZ 833013 » **SATNAV:** GOATHLAND
START/FINISH: GOATHLAND » **PARKING:** CAR PARK IN GOATHLAND VILLAGE (PAY AND DISPLAY)
CAFÉ: GOATHLAND TEAROOMS TEL: 01947 896446 » **PUBLIC HOUSE:** THE MALLYAN SPOUT HOTEL TEL: 01947 896486, THE GOATHLAND HOTEL TEL: 01947 896203, THE INN ON THE MOOR TEL: 01947 896296 (ALL IN GOATHLAND)

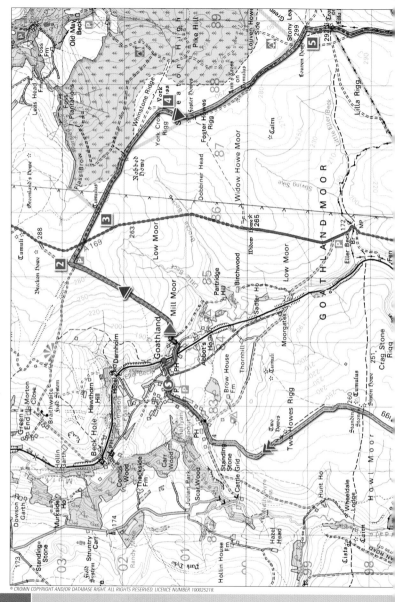

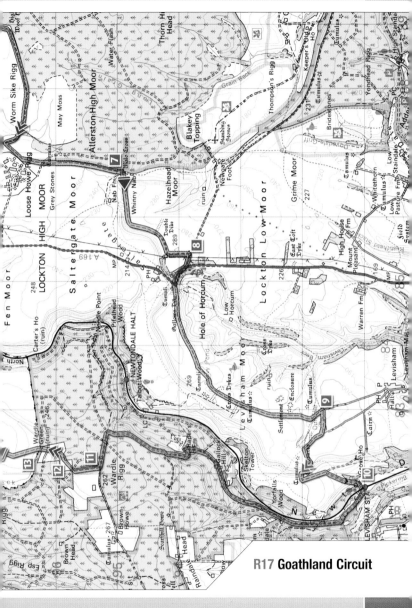

R17 Goathland Circuit

Directions — Goathland Circuit

↪ Turn **R** out of the car park and **L** at road junction. Follow the road past the station, over the bridge and up the hill.

2 About 600m before this road meets the A169 turn **R** at moors info board onto a doubletrack bridleway. After 400m go **SA** at gate over road and **SA** at gate onto firm bridleway.

3 Follow wide doubletrack bridleway past bridleway to left after 500m. **SA** at junction where track drops to fence corner. **SA** at double gate with fence to right and forest on left.

4 Keep **R** at next junction after short climb, *Bridleway* sign on left. Use track in heather on right to avoid ruts. **SA** at the left hand double gate keeping fence to right.

5 Turn **R** at top of hill onto firm gravel track and immediately go through gate. Follow firm track for 1.6km to gate at forest edge. **SA** at gate and keep **R** at next junction after 500m. Stay with this track following the forest edge for 2.5km to gate just before the Fylingdales complex. Go **SA** at gate onto concrete road down sharp drop, over ford followed by a short and steep climb. After the climb continue for another 150m to a wide grassy area on left and *Bridleway* sign on right.

6 Turn **L** here through single gate onto grassy track with fence on left and orange post markers on right. After 350m turn **L** onto singletrack at fence corner. Cross **SA** over road after 300m still singletrack a little technical at first developing into soft grassy track and fence still to left. **SA** at single gate at 500m and continue along wide grassy track to gate at Malo Cross.

7 Turn **R** after gate onto wide singletrack with fence to right angling up the hillside. Track leads onto the plateau and doubletrack to gate. **SA** at gate swinging to the right and small forest. Go through gate and turn **L** onto singletrack along forest edge. Turn **R** after gate along edge of forest for 350m to wide hard track. Turn **R** to A169.

8 Cross the road carefully onto singletrack on far side. Turn **R** and follow to gate leading onto Levisham Moor. Ignore *No Cycling* signs – this is a legal right of way. A short climb leads to some easy wide track riding for 3km to Dundale Pond and a left bend. Keep with the main track uphill between the gorse for 200m.

9 Turn **R** at wall corner (*Bridleway* sign on wall) onto grassy track up short climb. Track stays with wall on left for 300m turning **R** again onto farm track (*Bridleway* sign) with wall on left for another 400m. Turn **L** at wall corner for another 160m. At wall corner keep **SA** ahead for 50m to hillside edge. Turn **R** onto singletrack downhill. (Track to left is footpath). Turn **L** at bottom onto wide track leading to road. Turn **R** at road, downhill to Levisham Crossing.

10 **SA** at crossing onto lane bending right into forest. Stay on this road for 3.7km to the junction after Raper's Farm. Turn **L** and follow the hairpin bends climbing sharply. 200m after the road levels turn **R** with the main road turning to dirt track. Stay with this track for 1km to sharp left-hand bend and a further 600m to field corner.

11 Turn **R** onto singletrack bridleway with hedge to left and trees to right. After 430m cross forest road and go through single gate into pasture. After 150m **SA** at second single gate and second field.

12 Keep to right of tree and **SA** at double gate. Drop down towards forest and bend left between two stone pillars. Cross track and keep to left of trees to gate leading to wooden bridge.

13 From the bridge follow singletrack uphill with some **G.O.A.P.** towards wall end. 20m after wall keep right at fork. **SA** crossing the track of the Lyke Wake Walk. Track goes double for a while past cairns to junction. Keep left here aiming for the Two Howes, 1km ahead. Stay with this track descending gently and bearing right dropping beside The Tarn. Follow track to far side bearing left with a short climb over ridge. Track bears right dropping to the road. Go **SA** on road into the village turning second **L** into car park.

18 Helmsley Circuit

Introduction

Unique within this guide, this is a 38km ride within the National Park, yet which doesn't cross any moorland. This route makes a pleasant change from the heather and bracken but with over 900m of ascent it is still a tough cookie. The scenery gets better and better as the ride progresses, and the grand finale is a rewarding 6km dash on forest trails down Riccal Dale, with beautiful views over into Bilsdale and across the moors to the north east.

The Ride

Ride out of Helmsley towards Harome, cross-country across streams and meadows to Sproxton. A long pull uphill towards Pry Rigg Plantation gains a lot more height than it seems, before a short, easy cruise through the forest brings on some tarmac riding with a brief sprint on the A170. The first downhill of the day arrives over Scawton Moor. The views open up for a long easy descent over grassland that finishes with a rocky drop into Ryedale. More tarmac and a number of short, steep climbs wriggle up the valley before the hardest climb of the day: the grassy spur from Barnclose Farm. A farm track leads back down into the valley before tackling the bridleway past Broadway Foot and Fairhill Farm makes for some easy riding. The last climb leads around the top edge of Rievaulx Moor on wide forest track, leading back to the A170 and the cafés of Helmsley.

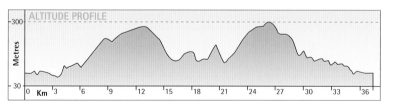

ALTITUDE PROFILE

Metres

HELMSLEY CIRCUIT   GRADE: ▲»▲

TOTAL DISTANCE: 38KM » **TOTAL ASCENT:** 977M » **START GRID REFERENCE:** SE 612838 » **SATNAV:** HELMSLEY
START/FINISH: HELMSLEY » **PARKING:** HELMSLEY OFFICIAL CAR PARK (EXPENSIVE) OR ROADSIDE EAST OUT OF THE TOWN.
CAFÉ: PLENTY IN HELMSLEY » **PUBLIC HOUSE:** HELMSLEY

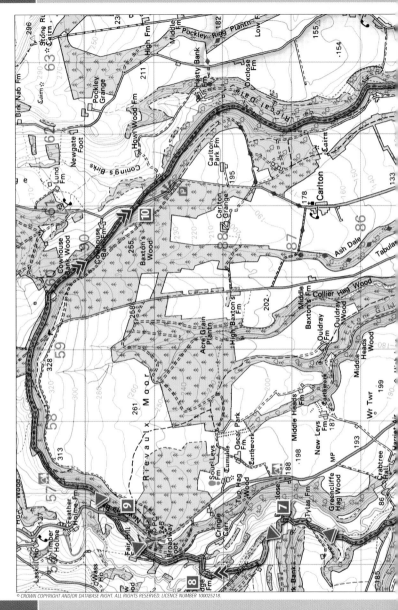

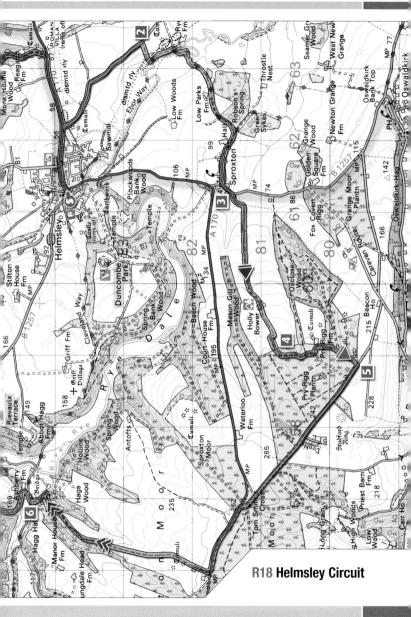

R18 Helmsley Circuit

Directions – Helmsley Circuit

➊ Head east from the square on the A170 for 1km and turn **R** into lane signposted *Harome*. Head down the lane for 1.5km and 50m after passing under telephone lines turn **R** onto bridleway.

➋ Ride to the bottom of the field and turn **L** under bridge to gate. Go through gate and keep **SA** to lane. Turn **R** onto lane and follow to the fish farm. Turn **R** before farm gate and then **L** along the fence for 200m. Turn **R** over footbridge. Go **SA** – aim for end of a line of trees. Keep trees to left leading to single gate. **SA** at gate for 50m and turn **L** at next gate. Go immediately **R** with hedge on right, leading to doubletrack to farm. Bear **L** before farm across field and through gate onto concrete track. Follow down dip and climb, joining track at far side of field. Turn **R** at T-junction to Sproxton.

➌ Turn **L** at main road and follow for 150m and turn **R** into lane. Follow the lane turning sharp **L** and then sharp **R** and on to Holly Bower Farm. Pass straight through the farmyard and onto doubletrack. After 400m turn **R** through gate and immediate **L** at trees. Follow to top of field making a quick **L** and **R** to forest gate. **SA** at gate onto forest road for 130m to junction.

➍ Turn **L** at junction, signposted *Bridleway* and follow for almost 500m and turn **L** towards Pry Rigg Farm. After 100 turn **R** just before the farm signposted *Bridleway*. Follow this track for almost 500m keeping right at junction and down to the sharp U-bend. Turn **R** here onto rough doubletrack (signposted *Bridleway*). Follow for 1km to the road.

➎ Turn **R** at road and follow for 2.7km to A170. Turn **L** onto A170 for a further 1km. 50m before the forest edge on the right turn **R** through gate onto bridleway. Go **SA** at farmyard through gate with fence on right. **SA** at next gate across open field. **NOTE:** Track is fairly indistinct. **SA** at single gate aiming to the left of trees ahead. Pass trees and **SA** at single gate and keep to right of gorse bushes. After 150m turn **L** at broken fence into the gully. **SA** at gates leading onto farm track and the farm road at the bottom of hill. Turn **L** and follow to road.

➏ Turn **R** at road and quick **L** over bridge. Follow this road around the bend and uphill. At the top the road bends left and then makes another short climb. Pass the bridleway on left and 100m further on turn **R** onto farm road with signpost for *Tylas Farm*. Follow for 1.4km to right bend and then left bend before Tylas Farm. Cross the stream and a short climb leads to Barn Close Farm. Turn **L** at the farm to gate.

7 SA at gate and follow a track up a grassy hill for 150m turning **R** with the wall. Stay with the wall on right for 260m and turn **L** for 100m. Turn **R** at wall corner and *Bridleway* sign. Follow for 200m to barn. At the barn turn sharp **R** onto track and ride 100m to gate. Go through the gate and follow track sharp **L** down the hill. Stay with this track ignoring first *Bridleway* sign on right to the next *Bridleway* sign just 50m before the farm gate. Turn **R** and drop down the field to wooden gate in the corner. Go through gate onto concrete farm road, turn **R** and follow to road.

8 Turn **R** at road and cross the bridge. Just 50m after the bridge turn **L** onto bridleway through woods. Keep **SA** joining a farm road and follow to Fairhill Farm. Just before the farm turn **R** onto singletrack bridleway (not signposted here) between two fences. After 160m turn **L** onto wider track after passing through gate. Follow this track keeping **SA** at gates to the road. Turn **R** at road and climb the hill for 150m and then turn **L** onto forest road with *Bridleway* sign.

9 Take this track climbing around the back of Rievaulx Moor. As the track turns right and south it begins to descend. The track through woods in Riccal Dale is well marked with *Bridleway* signs. Keep **R** at first fork to road after 180m.

10 Turn **L** and quick **R** onto bridleway, take **L** fork after 900m and **L** fork after 2km. Take **R** fork after 360m up a short climb and **L** fork after another 360m. Track starts to deteriorate but remains rideable to gate to field. **SA** at gate and cross the field to gate onto road. Turn **R** at road for 2km ride back into Helmsley.

SECTION 4

Killers

*They shouldn't actually kill you
but they will certainly wear you out,
building character in the process.
Allow plenty of time, make sure you're
well prepared and fuelled and then
have it. Give it 100% and that's what
you'll get back – big country rides
that reward hard work.*

Killers

sponsored by **GORE** BIKE·WEAR

19 The Seven Dales

Introduction

A testing ride based around seven valleys to the north of the moors, this route combines sections from others in the book, but also throws in a few stretches of off-road riding that have had little coverage in other guides. The climbs vary and are generally on tarmac or firm track, providing a reasonably fast shuttle to the more interesting off-road riding. Likewise, the road links are inevitable, yet provide a little respite for the legs and cover ground fast. Fuel up, pick a nice day and see if you've got what it takes...

The Ride

Bringing together some of the best riding the moors has to offer, **The Seven Dales Killer Loop** combines elements of the **Danby & Pannierman's Causeway** ride on page 7 and the **Kildale Ring** on page 35, among others. Starting conveniently from the Danby Lodge car park, the route climbs over the moor and has us visiting Danby Dale, Esk Dale, Glaisdale, Great Fryup Dale, Westerdale, Baysdale and Kildale. We finish with fine sea views from the bridleway on Gerrick Moor above Danby and the unusual singletrack of the Pannierman's Causeway. A long and demanding ride, but one not to be missed if you've got the legs for it.

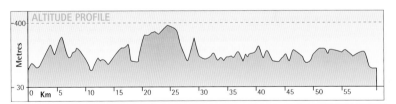

THE SEVEN DALES | GRADE: ▲

TOTAL DISTANCE: 61.5KM » **TOTAL ASCENT:** 1893M » **START GRID REFERENCE:** NZ 717084 » **SATNAV:** YO21 2NB
START/FINISH: DANBY LODGE CAR PARK » **PARKING:** DANBY LODGE CAR PARK (PAY AND DISPLAY)
CAFÉ: THE MOORS TEAROOM, DANBY LODGE TEL: 01287 660362; STONEHOUSE BAKERY, DANBY TEL: 01287 660006; GLEBE COTTAGE TEAROOM, KILDALE TEL: 01642 724470 » **PUBLIC HOUSE:** DUKE OF WELLINGTON, DANBY TEL: 01287 660351; THE CLEVELAND INN, COMMONDALE TEL: 01287 660214

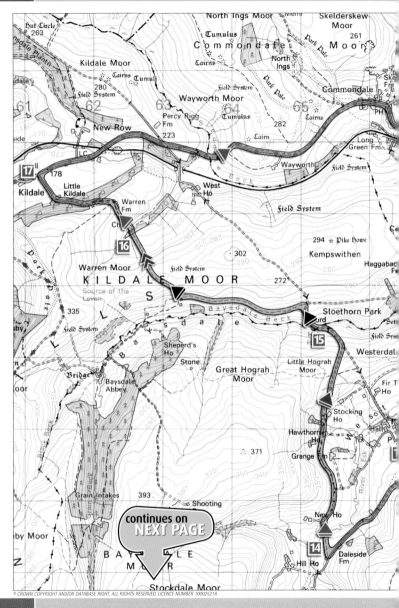

continues on
NEXT PAGE

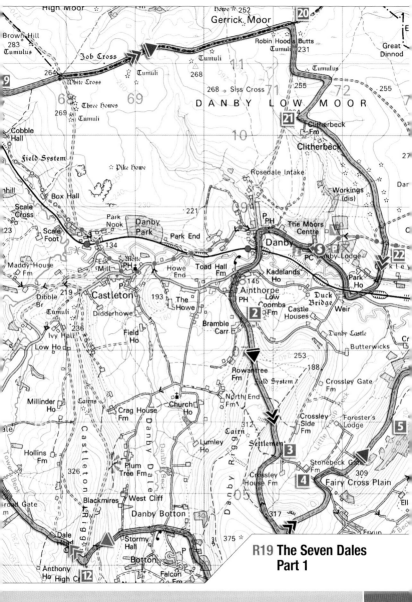

**R19 The Seven Dales
Part 1**

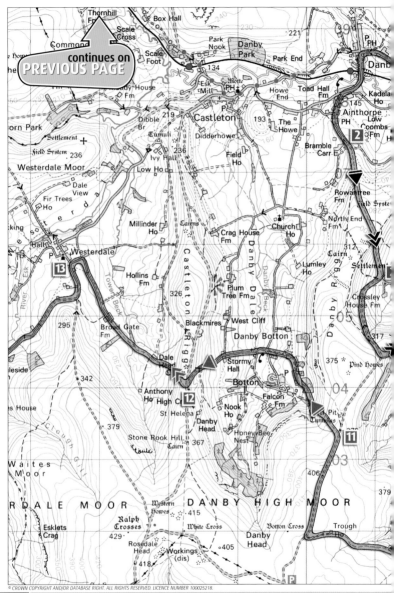

continues on PREVIOUS PAGE

Directions – The Seven Dales

➲ Turn **R** out of the car park and follow the road into Danby village. At the crossroads turn **L**. Cross the bridge into Ainthorpe and turn **L** up lane signposted *Fryup*.

2 Ignore the first bridleway on the right after the village and pass the tennis courts turning **R** at the next bridleway at the road bend. Multiple tracks lead to a gate. **SA** at gate and follow the eroded track over Ainthorpe Rigg. 1km after the gate keep **SA** and follow the track down the first descent; technical at first with easy run-out to the road.

3 Turn **R** at the road, signposted *Rosedale*. Climb the hill for 1.4km to a point where the road bears right. Turn **L** onto singletrack bridleway (*Bridleway* sign over rock) bending to left past a seat and dropping into a shallow gully. Go **SA** at gate to right. Keep to singletrack to right of gully passing a drop to the right and then sweeping down a grassy track to gate. Now aim to the right of the 'Roundhill'. **Note:** Track here is fairly indistinct. Go **SA** at next gate, aiming for the building towards the left and the gate to the road.

4 Turn **L** at road and then after 300m turn **R** onto farm doubletrack bridleway. At 300m turn **R** again onto climb between two walls. After 200m turn **L** through gate still climbing with wall to left. **SA** at gate at top and follow wall to corner. Here three tracks open up. (**Caution:** The left singletrack is easy to follow but is not a legal right of way.) Take the wider, central grassy track and follow this carefully over the moor. It is all rideable and can be navigated. Aim to the right of two trees and then the wall corner to the left.

5 Turn **R** through gate (50m to the right of footpath gate). Keep wall to left and follow singletrack along the top of Danby Crags, **SA** at all gates. It can get quite boggy at the last gate. Follow the track to wall corner near farm and join farm road. Turn **L** and follow to road junction.

6 Turn **L** onto the road and follow for 2.5km, following all signs for *Glaisdale*. After the crossroads on Lealholm Lane the road makes two sweeping bends. The second bend drops and then makes a short climb, meeting a wall at a sharp bend.

7 Turn **R** here onto a gravel double bridleway. Pass house to left, **SA** at junction with track to gate. Continue through gate onto double grassy track with fence to left. Leave fence corner following the track onto the ridge joining the main Glaisdale Rigg track in a shallow valley.

8 Turn **R** onto the firm Rigg track, ignoring the bridleway ahead, and follow this for just over 2km to the fourth bridleway off to the left. Turn **L** at metal *Bridleway* sign onto grassy doubletrack down to wall corner. **SA** on singletrack, then doubletrack to left bend and then singletrack through the ferns with wall to left on final descent to the gate at the bottom.

9 Turn **R** on the valley road and follow this all the way up the head of the valley to the T-junction at the top of a stiff climb. Turn **R** onto road for 300m.

10 Turn **L** onto bridleway and follow rocky singletrack around the head of the valley, past Trough House shooting lodge to the road at the far side. Turn **R** for 1.5km to a bridleway on the left.

11 Turn **L** onto singletrack bridleway across the heather, dropping gradually. Go **SA** at crossed tracks into doubletrack gully, boggy in parts. Gully bends to right with drop-offs and then bends left. Turn **R** at track at bottom of gully towards double gate under tree at corner of Danby reservoir (Big Iron Tub). **SA** across field to single gate and then double gate into forest. Stay with main track (cobbles). After 200m follow track sharp **L** downhill and then turn **R** at bottom onto soft track. Go **SA** at gate with building on right and then double gate, leading into lane. Follow lane downhill to join valley road, keeping **SA**, and then onto steep climb up west side onto the Castleton/Hutton-le-Hole road.

12 Cross the road and go straight onto a singletrack bridleway. Follow down to the gate at Dale Head Farm. Pass through the gate and turn **L** at tree and sign and pass between two buildings. Turn **R**, pass farmhouse and take **R** fork to gate at corner of wall. **SA** at gate and after 100m ride between wall and hedge. **SA** with wall on left for 150m to sharp **R** turn at the bottom of field. Follow track with stream on left for 30m turning **L** over bridge to gate. **SA** and short climb to gate. **SA** again with wall to left. Ride for 100m and **SA** at gate with wall on right and **SA** at farm gates onto farm lane. 800m after joining the farm turn **L** at the junction and then **L** in Westerdale village.

13 Follow the road up a bank for 500m and turn **R** into a lane. Pass the pumping station to the right and continue for another 1.4km. Turn **R**, 50m after building on left (*Bridleway* sign on left under tree), through gate into enclosure and **SA** at opposite gate into field. Cross the field, keeping fence to left. **SA** at single gate in corner of field. Follow doubletrack left and then right and over ford. Turn **L** to to climb to double gate at wall corner. Follow the wall to the right and the double gate leading onto the farm lane.

14 Turn **R**. After 500m the track bends sharp right through metal gate. Keep **SA** on doubletrack with wall to right. At 300m track bends left. 30m after left bend, turn **R** onto grassy track. Go through double gate with white marker for Esk Valley Walk and keep wall to right. **SA** at next two gates and ride through the middle of field. At bottom of slope join doubletrack past Hawthorn House. Go through the iron gate down the bank onto farm track. **SA** at gate uphill onto the John Breckon Road. Keep with this lane for 800m and turn **L** at junction. Drop down to the ford at Hob Hole.

15 Keep **SA** from the ford up a steep climb to a bridleway on the left opposite the road to Castleton. Turn **L** onto the bridleway. After almost 2km turn **R** at a barn onto singletrack and a short, steep climb. **SA** at gate on ridge, followed by a nice section of singletrack down to a gate in the wall.

16 **SA** at gate across a soft field and **SA** at next gate turning **L** past the chimney. **SA** at another gate and climb farm track up steep bank past Warren Farm and ride through the gate onto the lane.

17 Turn **R** on road to east of Kildale and follow for 5.6km to Commondale. Turn **R** at The Cleveland Inn onto lane. After left bend turn off the lane through the gate onto bridleway (essentially **SA**). Follow this bridleway around left bend and then right bend. 150m after the next gate turn **L** up a grassy bank to a gate (opposite footpath gate on right).

18 Pass through the gate onto a wide grassy track keeping the wall to the left. The track becomes a more defined singletrack. After 180m cross a ditch and the track starts to bear more to the right and steeply uphill to a single gate in the wall on the horizon. (Top right corner with wire fence). Pass through the gate and turn **R** onto singletrack with a little pavement. After 50m the track bears left away from the wall onto a wide doubletrack. There is a boulder here on each side of the track. (**SA** would lead you into a bog!) Follow to the road.

19 Turn **R** onto the road and continue to the T-junction. Continue **SA** onto another bridleway that begins with broken tarmac changing to sandstone further on. As you climb over the first brow the view to the NE opens up over towards Boulby potash mines and the North Sea. Continue on this track past Siss Cross Hill to the Danby road.

20 Turn **R** at the road and then after 650m at brow of hill turn **L** onto narrow tarmac lane. Follow this lane for 600m into the 'saddle'. A *Bridleway* sign on the left marks the point where the bridleway crosses the road. Turn **R** onto a singletrack (Pannierman's Causeway) in a shallow gully and follow this track as it bears first SW and then S towards Clitherbeck Farm. This track soon becomes pavement and leads onto the bridleway near the farm. Watch out for the ditches at the end of the pavement and just before the farm.

21 Turn **L** onto the bridleway and continue **SA** ignoring the right turn to the farm. At the bottom where the track bears right (footpath) leave the track and go **SA** picking up a singletrack to the right of a shallow gully. Stay on this track to rejoin the main track after 170m. Turn **L** and follow to road. At the road go **SA** to T-junction.

22 Go **SA** through the gate opposite and down a wide, rough doubletrack, walled on both sides. Turn **R** at the bottom onto a narrow lane and follow this under the railway to another junction. Turn **R** and follow the road back to the car park.

20 The Best Western

Introduction

A 77km ride, 87% of which is off-road, and with over 2000m of ascent this route really is a killer. The climbs are short but numerous, with Kepwick Bank and the singletrack up Cold Moor being the toughest. There is over 10km of singletrack, plus long descents and some particularly tricky downhills. From the start over in the Hambleton Hills, across to the typical moorland terrain above Bransdale and the final few miles over the distinctive Cleveland Hills, wherever you are on this route you will be presented with a vast panorama of some of the best views that this corner of England has to offer.

The Ride

You'll be thinking that starts don't come much easier than this as you blast down Silton Forest, but be warned... you pay for it soon as you hit Kepwick Bank. From then on it's up and down all the way round! Enjoy.

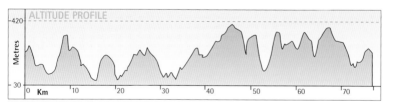

THE BEST WESTERN   **GRADE:** ▲

TOTAL DISTANCE: 77KM » **TOTAL ASCENT:** 2200M » **START GRID REFERENCE:** SE 479959 » **SATNAV:** OSMOTHERLEY
START/FINISH: SQUARE CORNER CAR PARK ABOVE OSMOTHERLEY   »   **PARKING:** SQUARE CORNER CAR PARK
CAFÉ: HAWNBY POST OFFICE TEAROOM TEL: 01439 798223; LORD STONES CAFÉ, CARLTON BANK TEL: 01642 778227;
PLUS MANY OTHERS... » **PUBLIC HOUSE:** THE INN AT HAWNBY, TEL: 01439 798202; PLUS MANY OTHERS...

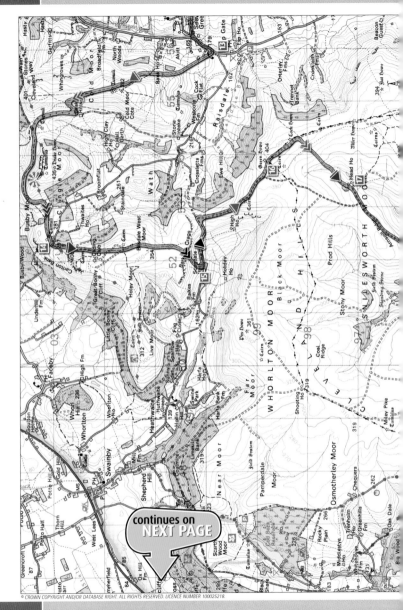

continues on
NEXT PAGE

R20 The Best Western
Part 1

continues on **PREVIOUS PAGE**

R20 **The Best Western**
Part 2

Directions – The Best Western

➋ Leave the car park turning **L** on a wide, firm track towards the climb up Black Hambleton. After 500m turn **R** at gate signposted *Route65*.

2 Follow this track into the forest and through to the gate at the bottom. The next junction is signposted *Kepwick 1¼m*. Ride towards Kepwick and after 2km, and just after a short climb, turn **L** at the next junction signposted *Unsuitable for motors*. Follow this road right to the top onto the Drovers' Road.

3 Turn **L** onto an extra wide track for almost 500m then turn **R** just before wall end onto a wide grassy track. (No markers – this turning is about 10m before the public footpath joins from the gate on left.) Follow this grassy track for 200m to a fork. Take **L** fork to gate.

4 Follow fence from gate on singletrack to wall corner where the track bears right to the top of a descent. Continue on boggy track across valley floor keeping **L** where singletrack joins doubletrack, and start climbing towards the forest. After 200m turn **R** through gate into forest. Keep **L** at doubletrack. At a point after 200m where four tracks cross keep **R** and down. Follow through right bend to Arden Hall. Turn **L** at end of building and **R** to lane.

5 Turn **L**, signposted *Hawnby*. Follow for 2km towards Hawnby and turn **R** at the next junction. Pass the buildings (tea room if required) and turn **R** at junction. Follow this lane up the hill until *25%* road sign. Turn **L** just after this sign onto a bridleway. (Sign on right). After 150m keep **R** at fork. After 750m keep **SA** joining forest road from left. After another 1.2km go **SA** at gate into field with fence to left.

6 Go through the gate and follow track sharp **L** down the hill. Stay with this track, ignoring first bridleway sign on right, to the next bridleway sign just 50m before the farm gate. Turn **R** and drop down the field to wooden gate in the corner. Go through gate onto concrete farm road, turn **R** and follow to road.

7 Turn **R** at road and cross the bridge. Just 50m after the bridge turn **L** onto bridleway through woods. Keep **SA** joining a farm road and follow to Fair Hill Farm. Just before the farm turn **R** onto singletrack bridleway (not signposted here) between two fences. After 160m turn **L** onto wider track after passing through gate. Follow this track, keeping **SA** at gates to the road. Turn **R** at road and climb the hill for 150m and then turn **L** onto forest road with *Bridleway* sign.

8 Follow this track, climbing around the back of Rievaulx Moor. As the track bears right and south it begins to descend. Stay with this track for 5.5km to the Helmsley-Bransdale road. Turn **L** for 1km. Turn **R** through gate onto indistinct bridleway keeping left of a group of trees. Keep **SA** towards stone wall with blue bridleway marker. At end of field track goes left and along stone wall. Go through gate keeping to line of fence on left dipping down to stream. Take bridleway **SA**. Track turns right as you climb through gate and joining farm track. Follow this track through Howl Wood Farm. Keep ahead at all gates to steep climb. Bear **L** at top of bank and follow track, bending right to road.

9 At road, cross **SA** to bridleway. Keep to right-hand edge of field, with fence to right, to single gate. Turn **R** at gate and follow singletrack downhill to stream. Climb hill at other side, crossing track, and continue **SA** at gate at top of climb. Keep hedge on your right up to the road. Turn **L** onto the road. Road ends after 1km – keep **SA** at gate onto doubletrack. After another 1km keep **SA** at gate at trees. At next gate take track to left and descend Rollgate Bank to moor.

10 Go **SA** at next two gates, the second after a pond. **SA** at double gate onto singletrack and follow this to the Bransdale road. Turn **R** for 1km and then turn **L** onto wide bridleway (at wooded signpost and a plaque – *Newton Tower Estate*). Follow this firm sandstone track for 2km to a left fork 100m after a stone pillar on left at short drop. Follow doubletrack for 2.5km over Slape Wath Moor and a steep drop into Tripsdale.

11 Cross stream onto a steep, zig-zag climb leading to the top of hill overlooking Bilsdale. Turn **R** at T-junction, still on wide track. After 300m keep left with a bend then right. Follow track for another 1km.

12 Turn **L** at small cairn 100m after stone pillar onto bridleway dropping to trees. Go through gate and follow singletrack to bend. Keep right with bend on wide track bending left to another junction. Turn **R** at bridleway sign onto partly gravelled track. Keep to track around a wide left-hand bend, dropping steeply after bend. Continue to wide forest track, turning **L** and quick **R** at *Bridleway* signs onto singletrack drop along edge of woods with fence to left. Single gate at end. Cross track and turn **L** to single gate and **R** onto firm track with wall to right. Follow this down to the barns. Keep **SA** at all gates onto farm lane. Cross ford at bottom and turn **L** onto lane. Turn **L** at lane end onto B1257. Follow road to Chop Gate. Turn **R** at junction signposted *Carlton in Cleveland* and then immediately **R** at bridleway sign onto track behind the chapel.

13 Follow the track between high hedges and go **SA** at track crossing and **SA** at following gates leading eventually onto singletrack. Keep to left of clay bank, away from wall. Follow the singletrack all the way to the top of the ridge. Turn **R** onto doubletrack and **L** at next junction onto steep descent. At bottom turn **R** with wall and follow to track at bottom. Turn **R** onto good track for 750m. Go **SA** at gate into open field aiming for wall corner and bridleway post. From the corner follow track to gate with wall on right. After gate turn **L** at Cleveland Way sign and after a short, paved track turn **R** at bridleway sign onto singletrack. Follow this track for 1.5km across the front of Cringle Moor to *Bridleway* sign. Turn **L** for 270m to gate. Go through gate and turn **R** onto wide track keeping **SA** at next gate towards the top of Carlton Bank. At wall corner keep straight ahead passing to the right of a copse of trees. After the trees turn **R** at wide track marked by three boulders. After 100m take **R** fork on grass track to gate and road. Turn **L** at the copse to visit Lord Stones Café if you require refreshment.

14 Cross the road bearing left onto firm, wide track, **SA** at gate and climb the bank for 830m to bridleway signpost at top bend. Turn **L** onto singletrack for 300m turning **L** again onto doubletrack. After 370m turn **L** at junction. Follow wide track for another 920m to junction just past 'Brian's Pond'. Turn **R** onto signposted singletrack bridleway for 400m to edge of Barker's Crags. Turn **L** onto singletrack for 100m (ignore track off to right) over rocky drop and bearing sharp right to single gate. After the gate drop down over boggy section to wall corner and then follow wall down to road. Turn **L**.

15 Go **SA** at iron gate and then turn **L** after 50m onto rough track signposted *No vehicles* and *Cycles* with an arrow. After 320m the track turns left up a wide rutted bank, bending right to gap in wall. After the gap follow doubletrack to gate at top. From the gate go **SA** on wide grassy track taking **R** fork to firm track. Turn **R** and follow this good track for 1.5km up a stiff climb to junction.

16 Turn **L** at junction and look out for a small pile of stones to the right of Cock Howe after 1100m. Turn **R** onto excellent singletrack. Follow it all the way down for 900m to a stream crossing. (Watch out for the hidden drop offs!) Cross the stream and stay with the singletrack, climbing up the other side and then crossing over a grassy area to a wall corner. Continue with the wall on the left and past the small woods to the right and join a wider track leading out of farm land to the left.

17 Turn **R** and follow this track all the way along Arnsgill Ridge and down through two gates to a narrow lane at Hill End Farm. Turn **R** on the lane and down to a gate onto another concreted lane. Turn **L** and continue over a cattle grid to Low Cote Farm at the road bend. From the farm go **SA** down the road.

> ***Alternatively**, turn **R** for a quicker/easier finish along the road.

18 At the bottom of the hill turn **R** over a stream and **SA** to gate with a sign for *Lower Locker Farm*. After the gate the farm track bends left; after the bend you will see a bridleway post on the right. Turn **R** here through a single gate and up a grassy field, with the fence on the left, to another gate leading to the moor.

19 This singletrack is easy to follow, heading straight for the old farm buildings at Dale Head. If visibility is good the buildings are always in view. As the track nears the buildings it drops to a small stream. Fork **R** before the drop. Cross the '*more than adequate*' bridge and then climb up a grassy field, clearly marked with *Bridleway* signs. Turn sharp **L** at the buildings and then **R** before the ruins. Continue on doubletrack through two gates. After 800m the track turns sharp right, crosses a stream and another gate leads to short climb to the road. Turn **L** on the road to return to the car park.

SECTION 5

Bonus Section

» *Pickering A–B*
» *Trail Centres*
» *Moors to Sea Cycle Network*
» *Top Tens*

Bonus Section
sponsored by

LUMICYCLE
High Performance Cycle Lights
www.lumicycle.com

21 Pickering—Levisham Station/ Goathland

10.3km
21.8km

Introduction

Making use of the North Yorkshire Moors Railway to give a one-way ride, this is easy mountain biking for a hot summer's day. Ride through fields above the preserved steam railway of the NYMR with an unexpected technical descent just above Levisham, before taking a steam train back to Pickering. Alternatively, continue off-road to Goathland and pick up the train there.

The North Yorkshire Moors Railway does allow bikes on their trains but available space varies. The maximum is usually about five. For more information visit www.nymr.co.uk or call 01751 472508.

The Ride

This is easy to follow. From Pickering Station, we take the road north to the first crossing and turn off onto a narrow lane leading to the bridleway for Blansby Park. We continue across fields of crops and a short forest section that leads to East Brow Road. Turning off this lane, we keep straight ahead and pick up the first downhill on Newton Banks. This leads us out into an opening with impressive views over Newtondale before we dip back into the woods for a little more technical downhill to the lane for Levisham Junction.

The longer link to Goathland sees us following forest tracks through the eastern edge of Cropton Forest taking in great views into Newtondale and finishing on 4km of singletrack over Simon Howe.

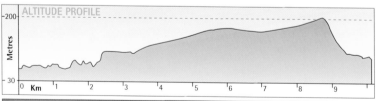

ALTITUDE PROFILE

Metres

200

30

0 Km 1 2 3 4 5 6 7 8 9

ROUTE NAME   **GRADE: ▲ » ▲**

TO LEVISHAM/GOATHLAND – DISTANCE: 10.3KM/ 21.8KM » **ASCENT:** 205M » **START GRID REFERENCE:** SE 796843
SATNAV: YO18 7AJ » **START/FINISH:** PICKERING STATION » **PARKING:** PICKERING STATION CAR PARK
CAFÉ: PLENTY IN PICKERING » **PUBLIC HOUSE:** PICKERING » **MORE INFORMATION:** WWW.NYMR.CO.UK

Directions – Pickering–Levisham Station/ Goathland

➔ From the railway station car park turn **L** onto road and follow for 1.4km to railway crossing. 50m after the railway crossing turn **R** into Blansby Park Lane.

2 Keep **SA** at gate with bridleway marker onto dusty road. Pass house to left and after 100m turn **L** through double gate with bridleway arrow onto singletrack lined with trees and bushes. This track climbs steadily. Keep **SA** at junction continue to gate at top into field.

3 From the gate keep to doubletrack left around edge of field. At field corner go through gate onto doubletrack heading for tree line. **SA** at gate on more doubletrack joining farm road. Keep **R** at fork before farm. Pass farm to left and **SA** at cattle grid with hedge to right. Keep **SA** at next farm following bridleway markers.

4 Follow track around farm and turn **R** though cut doubletrack though a crop field. Follow this track for 1.1km to forest edge. Go **SA** between posts into forest and then **SA** at gate onto doubletrack with hedge to left and fence to right. At 200m go **SA** at two gates past farm. **SA** at gate onto rough tarmac lane.

5 Stay on this lane for 1.2km to a point where the lane bends sharp left. Go **SA** onto wide rough track. (No signposts). At 500m look out for public footpath sign on left.

6 Then after 200m opposite an iron gate, turn **R** down singletrack. The track widens as it descends. Keep to right-hand singletrack to avoid the soft stuff. **SA** at gate at bottom keeping to the top of the field. Drop to gate and **SA** onto singletrack between trees and bushes. As track drops into gully keep to track on right to gate at bottom. Follow track over stream bending right to forest road.

7 Turn **R** to Levisham Station and catch the steam train back to Pickering.

←⊙⊙ Making a day of it

You can also join Route 17 **Goathland Circuit** on page 101 at Instruction 10 to continue to Goathland.

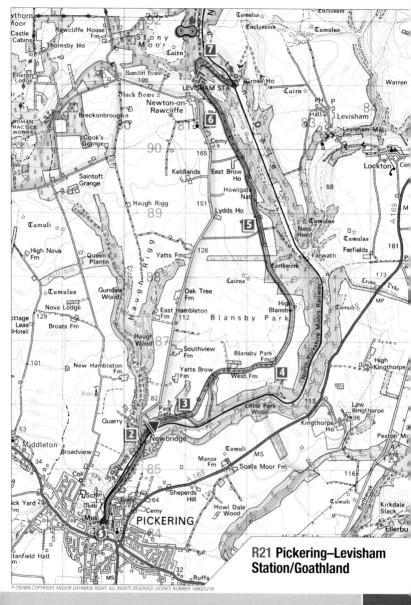

R21 Pickering–Levisham Station/Goathland

north york moors *trail centres*

As well as the tremendous natural riding on the moors, the national park is also home to two of the UK's trail centres. Dalby, in the south east is the largest purpose-built trail centre in England, and Guisborough Forest in the north west is a smaller centre with two waymarked trails.

Dalby

As you'd expect from England's largest trail centre, there's something here for all riders. There are two green routes, a blue, a long red (37km and nearly all singletrack), a technical black and the Dixon's Hollow Bike Park.

The trails

The two green-graded trails at Dalby (the 3km **Ellersway Family Cycle Route** and the 10km **Adderstone Cycle Trail**) have no nasty surprises, giving pleasant cycling on wide trails. The 14km **Blue** route steps things up a little bit, giving sections of singletrack riding but, as with much of the riding at Dalby, it lacks any significant climbs or descents due to the landscape of the area.

The **Red** route at Dalby is long – 37km to be precise, the vast majority of which is singletrack. As the lie of the land is undulates, with little steep terrain, this route requires a fair bit of pedalling and consequently can be tiring. That said it's a fine example of good trail centre single-track. Best started from the lower car park.

Although only 10km long (OK that is fairly long – it just feels short after the Red) Dalby's **Black** route is a full-on technical assault requiring a full set of riding skills. Should you need to polish your riding skills in preparation for the black, then the **Dixon's Hollow Bike Park** is not a bad place to start.

Getting there

From Pickering, follow the A169 north towards Whitby, turning right just before the Fox and Rabbit Pub onto the Thornton-le-Dale road. The Forest Drive is on your left after 2.5km.

Grid Ref: **SE 857 873**   Satnav: **YO18 7LT**

Facilities

Car parking (but £7 to access the toll road); toilets; bike shop; bike hire; café; visitor centre.

More information

Purple Mountain Bike Centre:
01751 460011
Dalby Visitor Centre: 01751 460295
www.forestry.gov.uk/dalbyforest

Guisborough

At the other end of the trail centre spectrum is Guisborough. With basic facilities and only two waymarked trails there's much less on offer here. If you're used to riding blue- or black-graded trails then you'll get something out of a visit, but the riding is technical and rooty, being situated on a steep forest hillside.

The trails

The 7km **Blue** route at Guisborough gives a good ride for technically less experienced riders, sticking predominantly to forest tracks. It does feature a fair bit of climbing however, so a degree of fitness is needed.

In contrast, the 12km **Black** route is a technical ride indeed; steep in places (particularly the initial forest road climb) with plenty of roots. It's also pretty worn which doesn't make it any easier to ride. Sections of the black are taken in on the **Pinchinthorpe** route (on page 11) and, on that ride or this, you'll see glimpses of some of the other unmarked singletrack riding hidden away in the woods.

Getting there

From Guisborough, head back towards Middlesbrough on the A171, turning left (south) onto the A173 towards Stokesley. Parking is as for Route 2 **Pinchinthorpe** (see page 11).

Grid Ref: **NZ 584 152** Satnav: **TS14 8HD**

Facilities

Free car parking; toilets; visitor centre

More information

Guisborough Visitor Centre: 01287 631132

Moors to Sea Cycle Network

The Moors to Sea long distance cycle network links together the North Yorkshire towns of Whitby, Scarborough and Pickering. An extension also links Great Ayton to Whitby via Danby.

The riding surfaces vary from disused railway lines, forest lanes and quiet lanes. Although the full network offers over 100 miles of riding, it can be broken into sections, suitable for families, leisure cyclists and less-experienced mountain bikers. Be aware that sections are quite remote and you should exercise caution in poor weather and riding conditions.

At the time of writing, much of the route is signposted however riders are advised to avoid relying entirely on signage. If you're interested in riding the Moors to Sea route we'd recommend picking up a set of route cards from the North York Moors National Park shop – available online at **www.visitnorthyorkshiremoors.co.uk**

More information
www.moortoseacycle.net
www.visitnorthyorkshiremoors.co.uk
North York Moors National Park
T: 01439 770657

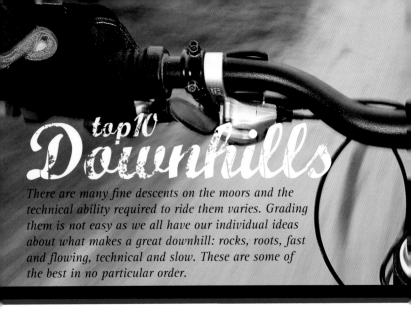

top 10 Downhills

There are many fine descents on the moors and the technical ability required to ride them varies. Grading them is not easy as we all have our individual ideas about what makes a great downhill: rocks, roots, fast and flowing, technical and slow. These are some of the best in no particular order.

1 Route 19 Little Fryup
GR NZ 710 044

This downhill gives technical riding in the gully and some exposure for a short while with a nice run off to the bottom.

2 Route 09 Whitestones – Boltby
GR SE 507 853

A gentle start from the escarpment edge under a larch-lined tunnel is followed by short but technical rock gardens and a long downhill run-out, finishing at the water splash before Boltby village.

3 Routes 08 & 14 Rudland Rigg – Farndale
GR SE 644 969

One of the best on the moors starting from a pile of rocks that think they make a cairn on Rudland Rigg. 1.5km of rolling, steady singletrack descent before the drop to West Gill Beck. Difficult to class this one – it's a great descent and a great singletrack!

4 Route 19 Glaisdale
GR NZ 744 043

Singletrack most the way and easy to ride for all with great views into the Glaisdale valley.

5 Route 20 Thorodale
GR SE 490 919

This one is tucked away and not easy to find even though it is a mere 500m from the busy drover's road. It's a short descent but singletrack and steep with some exposure.

Route 15 Fryup Head   GR NZ 714 016

One of the most technical downhills on the moors. Starting from the bridleway at the head of Fryup, the sweet singletrack makes as if it is going to launch you over the edge before somehow making a sudden left and picking a line between the rocks below. A run-out into the valley allows the pulse rate to return to normal.

Route 20 Scugdale   GR NZ 520 003

From the top of Barker's Crags this is a lovely singletrack drop through the bracken.

Route 13 Reversed Black Hambleton   GR SE 480 941

After some testing rocky sections at the top this is a fast, sweeping, wide track descent all the way back to the car park, with intermittent drainage mounds for you to practice your jumps.

Route 10 Rudland Rigg to Baysdale   GR SE 634 975

A fast but safe descent that anyone can ride. Take it as hard or as easy as you want on firm, wide doubletrack with fantastic views into the valley below.

Routes 07 & 19 Crossley Side (Ainthorpe Rigg)   GR NZ 710 061

After tackling the eroded track over Ainthorpe Rigg this is just reward. Watch out for the rock steps near the top before a quick blast into Fryup.

top10
Singletrack

Singletrack on the moors tends to be soft after rain so try and ride when the tracks are dry to get the best out of them. They are suitable for most abilities with more techie stuff thrown in here and there to really keep you on your toes. As with the Top 10 Downhills, the following are in no particular order.

Route 11 Rosedale South
GR SE 733 942 – SE 742 907

Written about many times, this famous stretch of moorland singletrack is sadly suffering from erosion diversions. Regardless, it's a measure of how good it is that it still makes a top ten singletrack ride. Best ridden when the bracken is tall.

Route 15 George Gap Causeway
GR NZ 702 005 – NZ 714 016

I'm always surprised that not many folk seem to know about this one. It's fairly level most of the way and starts along a 6 inch gap in the heather. Like others on the moors, the paved causeway is unusual to ride and offers a few technical challenges along the way.

Routes 13 & 20 Arnsgill – North of Bilsdale mast
GR SE 543 981 – SE 533 971

Not a well-known track but a wonderful 600m stretch of downhill riding. Watch out for the 'hidden' drops and the last drop to the gill. The track continues as singletrack after the short climb from Arnsgill.

Route 20 Reversed Cold Moor – Chop Gate
GR NZ 551 023 – NZ 556 003

Who could complain about 2km of singletrack, off-road descent? This is singletrack for all riders.

Route 10 Urra Moor
GR NZ 578 030 – NZ 578 030

Best ridden north to south from Carr Ridge above Clay Bank, or ride it heading north as part of the Clay Bank route. 2.7km of varied singletrack traversing the edge of Urra Moor. (Take care crossing the beck!)

Route 09 Whitestone Scar – Boltby Scar
GR SE 507 838 – SE 506 867

3km of singletrack bliss along the escarpment edge. Slightly more downhill south to north with great views over to the west. The only drawback is that it can get quite busy.

Route 17 Simon Howe Rigg – Goathland
GR SE 824 962 – NZ 826 006

Over 2.5km of singletrack, broken only occasionally with double track. Either way is good but if you finish at Blawath Beck the only way is up! Beware it is very energy sapping when wet – you have been warned.

Route 01 Pannierman's Causeway
GR NZ 718 107 – NZ 713 102

Short but sweet. Hats off to the monks for laying the path we now ride!

Route 20 Cringle Moor
GR NZ 531 031 – NZ 545 034

One to ride when it's dry. Ridden in either direction it gives cruising joy, but I think it's slightly better taken west to east. Better still, combine this with the great downhill to Kirby.

Route 04 Brown Rigg (near Danby Beacon)
GR NZ 743 093 – NZ 745 108

Narrow singletrack, dropping gently for 1.5km, with great views out over the North Sea.

Appendices

Tourist Information Centres

Danby	T: 01439 772 737
Great Ayton	T: 01642 722 835
Guisborough	T: 01287 633 801
Helmsley	T: 01439 770 173
Middlesbrough	T: 01642 729 700
Northallerton	T: 01609 776 864
Pickering	T: 01751 473 791
Redcar	T: 01642 471 921
Saltburn	T: 01287 622 422
Scarborough	T: 01723 383 636
Sutton Bank	T: 01845 597 426
Thirsk	T: 01845 522 755
Whitby	T: 01723 383 637
York	T: 01904 550 099

Weather

www.meto.gov.uk
www.metcheck.com
www.bbc.co.uk/weather

Food and Drink

Cafés

Forge Tea Shop
Hutton-le-Hole
T: 01751 417 444

The Lastingham Grange Hotel
T: 01751 417 345

Sutton Bank Visitor Centre
T: 01845 597 426

The Moors Tearoom
Danby Lodge
T: 01287 660 362

Stonehouse Bakery
Danby
T: 01287 660 006

Shepherds Hall
Lealholm
T: 01947 897 361

Glebe Cottage Tearoom
Kildale
T: 01642 724 470

Hawnby Post Office Tearoom
T: 01439 798 223

Chequers Tearoom
nr Osmotherley
T: 01609 883 710

Coffee Pot
Osmotherley
T: 01609 883 536

Ravenscar Tearooms
T: 01723 870 444

Abbey Tearoom and Store
Rosedale Abbey
T: 01751 417 475

Molly's Farm Shop and Tearoom
Rosedale Abbey
T: 01751 417 468

Goathland Tearooms
T: 01947 896 446

Pubs

The Lion Inn
Blakey Ridge
T: 01751 417 320

The Blacksmiths Arms
Lastingham
T: 01751 417 247

The Feversham Arms
Church Houses
T: 01751 433 206

The Whitestonecliffe Inn
Sutton-under-Whitestonecliffe
T: 01845 597 271

Duke of Wellington
Danby
T: 01287 660 351

The Cleveland Inn
Commondale
T: 01287 660 214

The Board Inn
Lealholm
T: 01947 897 279

The Cleveland Inn
Commondale
T: 01287 660 214

Queen Catherine Hotel
Osmotherley
T: 01609 883 209

The Golden Lion
Osmotherley
T: 01609 883 526

The Inn at Hawnby
T: 01439 798 202

The Millburn Arms
Rosedale Abbey
T: 01751 417 312

The New Inn
Cropton
T: 01751 417 330

The Bay Horse
Great Broughton
T: 01642 712 319

The Buck Inn
Chop Gate
T: 01642 778 334

The Mallyan Spout Hotel
Goathland
T: 01947 896 486

The Goathland Hotel
T: 01947 896 203

The Inn On The Moor
T: 01947 896 296

The Moorcock Inn
Langdale End
T: 01723 882 268

Accommodation

For youth hostels, visit www.yha.org.uk.
There are hostels in the following places on
or near the routes described:

Boggle Hole	
(nr Robin Hood's Bay)	T: 0870 770 5704
Helmsley	T: 0870 770 5860
Lockton (nr Pickering)	T: 0870 770 5938
Osmotherley	T: 0870 770 5982
Scarborough	T: 0870 770 6022
Whitby	T: 0870 770 6088

Camping

There is a variety of campsites available on and
around the moors depending on what you're
looking for. The following websites should provide
a good start for information, or alternatively
contact a local Tourist Information Centre.

www.enjoyengland.com
www.camping.uk-directory.com
www.find-a-campsite.co.uk
www.ukcampsite.co.uk

Hotels, Self-Catering and B&B

The **Park House Bed & Breakfast** at Ingleby Cross, just off the A172, comes highly recommended; bike friendly, nice spot, good food on offer and licensed bar.

Park House Bed & Breakfast
Ingleby Cross
North Yorkshire DL6 3PE
T: 01609 882 899   www.parkhousebb.co.uk

Another popular stop is **The Lion Inn** on Blakey Ridge, although you'll have to book well in advance as it's on the Coast to Coast.
T: 01751 417 320

For details of other accommodation, your best bet is to contact the **Tourist Information Centre** nearest to where you plan to ride.

Bike Shops

Westbrook Cycles
Stokesley
T: 01642 710 232   www.westbrookcycles.co.uk

Bike Traks
Great Ayton
T: 01642 724 444   www.biketraks.com

Bike Scene
Guisborough
T: 01287 610 735   www.bikescene.co.uk

Cowley Cycles
Northallerton
T: 01609 776 656   www.cowleycycles.co.uk

Yarm Cycles
Yarm
T: 01642 784 269   www.yarmcycles.net

GLG Cycles
Thornaby
T: 01642 674 273   www.glgcycles.co.uk

Dr Cranks Bike Shack
Whitby
T: 01947 606 661

Pickering Cycle Centre
Pickering
T: 01751 472 581

Grip Cycles
Scarborough
T: 01723 586 565   www.gripcycles.co.uk

The Bicycle Works
Scarborough
T: 01723 365 594

Bike-It Ltd
Scarborough
T: 01723 507 332

Scarborough Cycle Centre
Scarborough
T: 01723 506 677

Richardson's Cycles
Scarborough
T: 01723 352 682

Cycle Life
Scarborough
T: 01723 354 901

Cycle Heaven
York
T: 01904 636 578   www.cycle-heaven.co.uk

Evans Cycles
York
T: 0870 165 1109

Bike Hire

Purple Mountain
Low Dalby
T: 01751 460 011   www.purplemountain.co.uk

Other Publications

Mountain Biking Trail Centres – The Guide
Tom Fenton, Vertebrate Publishing

Yorkshire Dales Mountain Biking – The North Dales *Nick Cotton, Vertebrate Publishing*

Yorkshire Dales Mountain Biking – The South Dales *Nick Cotton, Vertebrate Publishing*

Off-Road Trails & Quiet Lanes: Cycling in the Lake District and Yorkshire Dales
Keith Bradbury, Vertebrate Publishing

The Author

Growing up in Teesside, Tony Harker started walking on the moors at a young age in the 1970s. Tony later discovered mountain biking in the 1990s following a history of knee problems and he is still going strong, even following a full knee replacement! Tony created the moors-dedicated mountain biking website **Muddybums** (www.muddybums.org.uk) in 1999 partly to hone his website-building skills and partly in response to the limited information of routes available to ride on the moors. The site has developed a good following, and Tony's passion for the moors and for riding shines through in this guide. When not riding, Tony runs **Fanatic Sport and Leisure** (www.fanaticsportandleisure.co.uk), the UK's leading retailer specialising in rowing clothing and accessories.

The Photographer

As well as being Vertebrate's Publishing Manager, John Coefield is also an accomplished photographer, with images regularly published in a variety of national publications, including **Climber Magazine** and numerous rock climbing guidebooks. John has been riding since a young age (although he has recently managed to shake off his childhood addiction to MBUK) and these days divides his time almost equally between riding, rock climbing and photography.
To view more of John's images visit:
www.johncoefield.com

Vertebrate Publishing

Vertebrate Publishing (VP) is the imprint of Vertebrate Graphics (VG), Britain's leading graphic design agency that specialises in the outdoor leisure market. Based deliberately near the Peak District, the guidebook production team spends as much time as they can walking, riding and climbing in the Peak District. We have had substantial success in the design and production of specialist outdoor books. These include *Hillwalking – The Official Handbook of the Mountain Leader and Walking Group Leader Schemes* (a bestselling outdoor title for three years running), highly praised rock climbing guidebooks such as *The Roaches – Staffordshire Grit* and the UK's best selling mountain bike guide: *Dark Peak Mountain Biking – True Grit Trails.*

VG create exciting graphic and web design and produce printed literature, advertising and websites, for more details of our services please refer to our website at: **www.v-graphics.co.uk** or e-mail us at: **info@v-graphics.co.uk**

MOUNTAIN BIKING GUIDEBOOKS

VERTEBRATE PUBLISHING

About the Great Outdoors

The great outdoors is not bottom bracket friendly; beautiful flowing singletrack can give way suddenly to scary rock gardens, hard climbs can appear right at the end of a ride and sheep will laugh at your attempts to clean your nemesis descent. Of course it's not all good news. You'll need a good bike to ride many of the routes in our set of mountain biking guides. You'll also need fuel, spare clothing, first aid skills, endurance, power, determination and plenty of nerve.

Bridleways litter our great outdoors. Our guides, written by local riders, reveal the secrets of their local area's best rides from 6 to 300km in length, including ideas for link-ups and night-riding options. Critically acclaimed, our comprehensive series of guides is the country's bestselling and most respected – purpose-built for the modern mountain biker.

The Guidebooks

Each guidebook features up to 28 rides, complete with comprehensive directions, specialist mapping and inspiring photography, all in a pocket-sized, portable format. Written by riders for riders, our guides are designed to maximise ride-ability and are full of useful local area information.

Available from bikeshops, bookshops or direct from:
www.v-publishing.co.uk

www.cotic.co.uk
07970 853 531

PHOTO: JOHN COEFIELD